PRINCIPLES OF THE NEW CHURCH.

PRINCIPLES

OF

THE NEW CHURCH:

SIGNIFIED BY

THE NEW JERUSALEM,

REVELATION XXI.

BEING A REPORT SUBMITTED TO THE EXECUTIVE COMMITTEE
OF THE GENERAL CONVENTION OF THE NEW CHURCH
IN THE UNITED STATES, JUNE, MDCCCLX.

NEW YORK:
PUBLISHED BY THE GENERAL CONVENTION OF THE NEW
JERUSALEM CHURCH IN THE UNITED STATES, AT
THE OFFICE OF ITS BOARD OF PUBLICATIONS,
346 BROADWAY.

JOHN L. JEWETT, AGENT.

1860.

RIVERSIDE, CAMBRIDGE:
STEREOTYPED AND PRINTED BY
H. O. HOUGHTON AND COMPANY.

REPORT.

To the Executive Committee of the General Convention:—

At the General Convention of the New Church in the United States, held in Philadelphia, June, 1856, the Executive Committee appointed Rev. Messrs. Stuart, Silver, Hibbard, Hayden, and the President of the Convention, Rev. Mr. Worcester, a Committee to prepare and present to the Executive Committee "a Declaration of Principles, Constitution, and Form of Government." The Committee presented a partial report at the Convention in Cincinnati, in June, 1857, and were continued. They again reported in part, at the Convention in Boston, June, 1858, and were again continued; and Rev. Mr. Benade was added to their number.

A meeting of the Committee was called at Philadelphia in October, 1858; and there were present Rev. Messrs. Stuart, Silver, Hibbard, and Benade. At this meeting the report was finished; and in order that it might be laid before the Executive Committee and the General Convention, the Committee determined to report in print. Their report was accordingly put to press in a pamphlet of seventy-two pages, 12mo. This report was laid before the Executive Committee, at the Convention in Philadelphia, June, 1859; and after due consideration, the whole subject was recommitted to the same Committee, with the addition of Rev. Messrs. Dike, Pettee, Hayward, Wilks, Giles, and Field. The Committee, thus constituted, were authorized to report in print; provided, that, "after due notice from the chairman, not less than three fourths of them meet and work together, and are unanimous."

This Committee met in Boston, October 26, 1859, pursuant to the call of the chairman; and there were present Rev. Messrs. Stuart, Silver, Hibbard, Hayden, Worcester, Benade, Dike, Pettee, Hayward, and Wilks. On the third day of the session, Rev. Mr. Benade was called away, and did not return to the Committee during its session. The Committee took up the subject *de novo*, and completed their work; and being unanimous, they determined to report in print.

The Committee were of opinion that the Declaration of Principles, Constitution, and Form of Government, ought to contain a summary view of the New Church *as an institution*, and a brief answer to the questions: What is the New Church? Whence came it? Upon what authority does it claim to be the New Church signified by the New Jerusalem in Revelation xxi.? What are its Doctrines? its Institutes of Order? and its Form of Government?

The Committee felt that their chief work was to collect and arrange into a Manual the materials already in use in the Church, and not to devise new materials. Consequently, the greater part of the following pages is extracted from the Word and the Writings of Emanuel Swedenborg. Indeed, the work entitled the "New Jerusalem and its Heavenly Doctrine" is made the basis of this *Declaration of Principles*. The translation of the extracts from Swedenborg has been carefully revised, and, as is hoped, essentially improved in many particulars.

The Committee humbly submit the result of their efforts; praying that this DECLARATION OF PRINCIPLES may be of use to the members of the New Church, and to others who would know its Doctrines, its Institutes, and its Forms of Order; and that it may aid in establishing the Church, and in promoting its peace and prosperity.

All of which is respectfully submitted.

In behalf of the Committee,

J. P. STUART, *Chairman.*

Boston, November, 1859.

CONTENTS.

ABBREVIATIONS.

A. C. The Heavenly Arcana, (Arcana Cœlestia.)
A. E. The Apocalypse Explained.
A. R. The Apocalypse Revealed.
C. Canons of the Entire Theology of the New Church.
C. L. Conjugial Love.
C. L. J. Continuation of the Last Judgment.
D. C. The Doctrine of Charity.
D. L. The Doctrine of the Lord.
D. L. W. Divine Love and Wisdom.
D. P. Divine Providence.
E. U. The Earths in the Universe.
F. The Doctrine of Faith.
H. D. The New Jerusalem and its Heavenly Doctrine.
H. H. Heaven and Hell.
L. The Doctrine of Life.
S. S. The Doctrine of the Sacred Scripture.
T. C. R. The True Christian Religion.
W. H. The White Horse.

PART I.

GENERAL DECLARATION.

PART I.

GENERAL DECLARATION.

CHAPTER I.

THE FAITH OF THE NEW HEAVEN AND THE NEW CHURCH.

FROM THE TRUE CHRISTIAN RELIGION OF EMANUEL SWEDENBORG.

THE Faith in the universal and the particular form is prefixed, that it may be as a Face before the work which follows; and as a Gate, through which entrance is made into a temple; and as a Summary, in which the particulars that follow are, each in its way, contained. It is said, *the Faith of the New Heaven and the New Church*, because heaven, where the angels are, and the church, in which men are, act as one, like the internal and the external in man: hence it is, that a man of the church, who is in the good of love from the truths of faith, and in the truths of faith from the good of love, is, as to the interiors of his mind, an angel of heaven; wherefore also he comes after death into heaven, and enjoys happiness there according to the state of the conjunction of those things. It is to be known, that in the New Heaven, which is at this day being established by the LORD, is this Faith, — the Face, the Gate, and the Summary of it.

THE FAITH OF THE NEW HEAVEN AND NEW CHURCH IN THE UNIVERSAL FORM IS THIS:

2. That the LORD from eternity, who is JEHOVAH, came into the world, that He might subjugate the hells, and glorify His Humanity: and that without this no mortal could be saved: and that they are saved who believe in Him.

3. It is said, *in the universal form*, because this is the universal of faith; and a universal of faith is that which must be in each and every thing of it. It is a universal of faith, that GOD is one in essence and in person, in whom is a Divine Trinity; and that the LORD GOD the SAVIOR JESUS CHRIST is He. It is a universal of faith, that no mortal could be saved, unless the LORD came into the world. It is a universal of faith, that He came into the world that He might remove hell from man; and that He did remove it by combats against it and by victories

over it: thus he subjugated it, and reduced it to order, and under obedience to Himself. It is a universal of faith, that He came into the world that He might glorify His Humanity which He took on in the world, that is, might unite it to the Divinity from which [it was]: thus He forever holds hell in order, and under obedience to Himself. Since this could not be done but by temptations admitted into His Humanity even to the last of them, and the last of them was the passion of the cross, therefore He underwent that. These are the universals of faith concerning the LORD.

4. The universal of faith on man's part is, That he should believe in the LORD: for by believing in Him conjunction is effected with Him, by which is salvation. To believe in Him is to have a trust that He saves; and since no one can have trust but he who lives well, this therefore is also understood by believing in Him. This the LORD also says in

John: "This is the will of the FATHER, that every one that believeth on the SON should have eternal life," vi. 40; and again: "He that believeth on the SON, hath eternal life: but he that believeth not the SON, shall not see life; but the anger of GOD remaineth upon him." iii. 36.

THE FAITH OF THE NEW HEAVEN AND NEW CHURCH IN THE PARTICULAR FORM IS THIS:

5. That JEHOVAH GOD is Love itself and Wisdom itself, or that He is Good itself and Truth itself: and that, as to the Divine Truth, which is the Word, and which was GOD with GOD, He descended and assumed the Humanity, to the end that He might reduce into order all things that were in heaven, and all things that were in hell, and all things that were in the church: since the power of hell then prevailed over the power of heaven, and on earth the power of evil over the power of good; and thence total damnation stood before the doors, and was

imminent. This impending damnation JEHOVAH GOD took away through His Humanity, which was the Divine Truth, and thus redeemed angels and men: and afterwards He united in His Humanity the Divine Truth to the Divine Good, or the Divine Wisdom to the Divine Love; and thus, together with and in the glorified Humanity, He returned into His Divinity in which He was from eternity. These things are understood by this in John: "The Word was with GOD, and GOD was the Word: and the Word was made flesh," i. 1, 14; and in the same: "I came forth from the FATHER, and came into the world: again I leave the world, and go to the FATHER," xvi. 28; and further by this: "We know that the SON of GOD has come, and has given us understanding, that we may know the TRUE ONE; and we are in the TRUE ONE, in His SON JESUS CHRIST. This is the true GOD and eternal life," First Epistle of John, v. 20, 21. From these things it is manifest, that without the LORD's coming into the world, no one could have been saved. It is the same at this day: wherefore, unless the LORD should again come into the world in the Divine Truth, which is the Word, not any one can be saved.

6. The particulars of the Faith on man's part are, 1, That GOD is One, in whom is a Divine Trinity; and that He is the LORD GOD the SAVIOR JESUS CHRIST: 2, That saving faith is to believe in Him: 3, That evils are not to be done, because they are of the devil and from the devil: 4, That goods are to be done, because they are of GOD and from GOD: 5, And that these are to be done by man as of himself; but that it is to be believed, that they are with him and through him from the LORD. The first two are of Faith; the next two are of Charity; and the fifth is of the conjunction of Charity and Faith, thus of the LORD and man. T. C. R. 1, 2, 3.

CHAPTER II.

ORIGIN OF THE NEW CHURCH.

THE SACRED SCRIPTURES announce the Second Coming of the LORD, to execute the LAST JUDGMENT, and to institute the NEW CHURCH, signified by the NEW JERUSALEM. The following declarations of the DIVINE WORD, among others, are the Foundation of our Faith in the NEW JERUSALEM, as a NEW DISPENSATION, and a NEW CHURCH:

AND I saw in the night visions, and behold, one like the SON OF MAN came with the clouds of heaven. And there was given unto Him dominion, and glory, and a kingdom; that all people, nations, and languages should serve Him. His dominion is an everlasting dominion, which shall not pass away; and His kingdom that which shall not be destroyed. Dan. vii. 13, 14.

AND JESUS went out, and departed from the temple: and His disciples came to Him to show Him the buildings of the temple. And JESUS said unto them, See ye not all these things? Verily I say unto you, There shall not be left here one stone upon another, that shall not be thrown down. And as He sat upon the Mount of Olives, the disciples came unto Him privately, saying, Tell us, when shall these things be? and what shall be the sign of Thy Coming, and of the Consummation of the Age?* And JESUS answered, and said unto them, Take heed that no one deceive you. For many shall come in my name, saying, I am CHRIST, and shall deceive many. And ye shall hear of wars, and rumors of wars: see that ye be not troubled: for all these things must come to pass; but the end is not yet. For nation shall rise against nation, and

* This is the true translation of the Greek text, Τῆς Συντελείας τοῦ αἰῶνος, erroneously rendered "*the End of the World.*"

kingdom against kingdom: and there shall be famines, and pestilences, and earthquakes in divers places. All these are the beginning of sorrows. Then shall they deliver you up to be afflicted, and shall kill you; and ye shall be hated of all nations for my name's sake. And then shall many be offended, and shall betray one another, and shall hate one another. And many false prophets shall rise, and shall deceive many. And because iniquity shall abound, the love of many shall grow cold. But he that shall endure unto the end, the same shall be saved. And this gospel of the kingdom shall be preached in all the world, for a testimony unto all nations; and then shall the end come. For then shall be great tribulation, such as was not from the beginning of the world to this time, no, nor ever shall be. Immediately after the tribulation of those days, shall the sun be darkened, and the moon shall not give her light, and the stars shall fall from heaven, and the powers of the heavens shall be shaken. And then shall appear the sign of the SON of MAN in heaven:

and then shall all the tribes of the earth mourn; and they shall see the SON of MAN coming upon the clouds of heaven, with great power and glory. Matt. xxiv. 1–14, 21, 29, 30.

THE seventh angel sounded; and there were great voices in heaven, saying, The kingdoms of this world are become our LORD'S and His CHRIST'S; and He shall reign for ever and ever. Apoc. xi. 15.

CONCERNING THE NEW HEAVEN AND NEW EARTH, AND WHAT IS UNDERSTOOD BY THE NEW JERUSALEM.

FROM THE NEW JERUSALEM AND ITS HEAVENLY DOCTRINE, BY EMANUEL SWEDENBORG.

It is said in the Apocalypse, —

"I saw a New Heaven and a New Earth; for the first heaven and the first earth had passed away. And I saw the Holy City, New Jerusalem, descending from GOD out of heaven, prepared as a Bride adorned for her Husband. And the city had a wall great and high, which had twelve gates; and on the gates twelve angels, and names written thereon, which are the names of the twelve tribes of

Israel. And the wall of the city had twelve foundations, in which were the names of the twelve apostles of the Lamb. And the city itself lay four-square, whose length was as great as the breadth. And he measured the city with a reed, twelve thousand furlongs; and the length and the breadth and the height of it were equal. And he measured the wall of it, a hundred and forty-four cubits,—the measure of a man, that is, of an angel. And the wall of it was of jasper; but the city itself was pure gold, like to pure glass: and the foundations of the wall of the city were of every precious stone. And the twelve gates were twelve pearls: and the street of the city was pure gold, as it were transparent glass. And the glory of God enlightened it; and the lamp of it was the Lamb. And the nations which were saved shall walk in the light of it; and the kings of the earth shall bring their glory and honor into it." xxi. 1, 2, 12–24.

THE man that reads these things understands them no otherwise than according to the sense of the letter; namely, that the visible heaven, with the earth, is to perish, and a new heaven to exist; and that upon the new earth is to descend the holy city Jerusalem; and that as to its measures it is to be according to the description. But the angels understand these things altogether otherwise; namely, everything spiritually which man understands naturally: and as the angels understand them, so they signify; and that is the Internal or Spiritual Sense of the WORD. By the New Heaven and New Earth, in the internal or spiritual sense in which the angels are, is understood a New Church, as well in the heavens as on the earth: by the city Jerusalem descending from GOD out of heaven, is understood its Heavenly Doctrine: by the length, breadth, and height, which were equal, are understood all the goods and truths of that Doctrine in the complex: by its wall are understood the truths that protect it: by the measure of the wall, which was a hundred and forty-four cubits, which is the measure of a man, that is, of an angel, are understood all those protecting truths in the complex, and their quality: by the twelve gates, which were of pearls, are understood introductory truths; and the same by the angels at the gates: by the foundations of the wall, which were of every precious stone, are understood the knowledges upon which that Doctrine is founded: by the twelve tribes of Israel are understood all things of the Church in general and in particular; and the same by the twelve apostles: by the gold like to pure glass, of which the city and street were built, is understood the good of love, out of which the doctrine shines forth with its truths: by the nations that are saved, and by the kings of the earth who shall bring glory and honor into it, are understood all from the church who are in goods and truths: by GOD and the LAMB is understood the

LORD as to the Divinity Itself and the Divine Humanity.

2. SUCH is the Spiritual Sense of the WORD, to which the natural sense, which is the sense of the letter, serves as the basis: but still these two senses, the spiritual and the natural, make one by correspondences. That there is such a spiritual meaning in all these things, there is not here leisure to show; since it is not the object of this work: but they may be seen shown in the "ARCANA CŒLESTIA."

3. BEFORE the New Jerusalem and its Doctrine are treated of, something will be said concerning the New Heaven and New Earth. In the small work on the "Last Judgment and the Destruction of Babylon," it was shown what is understood by the first heaven and first earth, which passed away; and after they passed away, thus after the last judgment was accomplished, a New Heaven was created, that is, formed, by the LORD. This Heaven was formed of all those, who, from the coming of the LORD even to this time, lived a life of faith and charity; since these only were forms of heaven: for the form of heaven, according to which all consociations and communications take place there, is the form of Divine Truth from Divine Good proceeding from the LORD; and this form man puts on as to his spirit, by a life according to Divine Truth. From these things it may be known of whom the New Heaven was made: hence also its quality; namely, that it is altogether unanimous: for he who lives a life of faith and charity, loves another as himself, and conjoins him to himself by love, and thus reciprocally and mutually; for, in the spiritual world, love is conjunction: wherefore, when all do the same, then from many, yea, from

innumerable ones consociated according to the form of heaven, there exists what is unanimous; and it becomes as it were one: for there is nothing that separates and divides, but everything conjoins and unites.

4. SINCE this Heaven was formed of all who were such, even from the time of the LORD to the present period, it is evident that it was formed of Gentiles as well as of Christians; but, for the greatest part, of the Infants of all in the universal world, who have died since the time of the LORD: for all these were received by the LORD, and brought up in heaven, and instructed by the angels, and then preserved, that, together with the rest, they might constitute the New Heaven. It may hence be concluded how great that Heaven is. That all who die infants are brought up in heaven, and become angels, may be seen in the work on "Heaven and Hell," n. 329–345; and that heaven is formed equally of Gentiles as of Christians, n. 318–328.

5. FURTHER as regards this New Heaven, it is to be known that it is distinct from the Ancient Heavens, namely, those which were before the coming of the LORD; but still, they with this are set in such order, that together they constitute One Heaven. The reason why this New Heaven is distinct from the ancient heavens is, that in the Ancient Churches there was no other doctrine but the Doctrine of Love and Charity; and they did not then know of any Doctrine of Faith separate: it is hence also, that the ancient heavens constitute higher expanses, but the New Heaven an expanse below them; for the heavens are expanses, one above another. In the highest expanse are they who are called Celestial Angels, the most of whom are from the Most Ancient Church: they who are there are called

celestial angels from celestial love, which is love to the LORD. In the expanse under them are those who are called Spiritual Angels, the most of whom are from the Ancient Church: they who are there are called spiritual angels from spiritual love, which is charity towards the neighbor. Under these are the Angels who are in the Good of Faith; who are those that lived a life of faith. To live a life of faith is to live according to the doctrine of one's church; but to live is to will and to do. Yet still, all those Heavens make one by mediate and immediate influx from the LORD. But a more full idea of those heavens may be had from the things which were shown in the work on "Heaven and Hell," and in the chapter there concerning the two Kingdoms into which the Heavens in general are distinguished, n. 20–28; and in the chapter on the Three Heavens, n. 29–40.

6. THUS far concerning the New Heaven: something will now be said of the New Earth. By a new earth is understood a New Church on the earth; since when a former church ceases to be, a new one is then instituted by the LORD: for it is provided by the LORD, that there is always a Church on the earth; since through the church there is conjunction of the LORD with the Human Race, and of Heaven with the world: for there the LORD is known, and there the divine truths are by which man is conjoined. That at this day a New Church is being instituted, see the small work on the "Last Judgment," n. 74. That a New Church is signified by the new earth, is from the Spiritual Sense of the WORD; for in that sense by earth is not understood any earth, but the nation itself therein, and its Divine Worship: for this is the spiritual meaning

of earth. Besides, by earth, without the name of a region adjoined, is understood in the WORD the land of Canaan; and in the land of Canaan there had been a Church from the most ancient times: whence it arose, that all the places which were therein, and which lay around on all sides, with the mountains and rivers, all which are named in the WORD, became representative and significative of such things as are the internals of the Church, which are what are called its spiritual things: hence it is, that, as it was said that by earth in the WORD is signified the land of Canaan, the Church also is signified; and the same here by the new earth. It comes from this, that it is usual in the church to say the Heavenly Canaan, and by it to understand Heaven.

7. WHAT is understood by Jerusalem in the WORD in its spiritual sense, shall also be told in few words. By Jerusalem is understood the Church itself as to Doctrine; and this for the reason that, in the land of Canaan, there, and not elsewhere, was the Temple, there the Altar, there Sacrifices were performed, and thus Divine Worship itself. Wherefore also three feasts were there celebrated yearly, and to them every male of the whole land was commanded to go. Hence then it is, that by Jerusalem in the spiritual sense is signified the Church as to Worship, or what is the same, as to Doctrine; for worship is prescribed in doctrine, and is performed according to it. Why it is said, "*the Holy City, New Jerusalem, descending from* GOD *out of Heaven*, is because by a city and a walled-town in the spiritual sense of the WORD is signified Doctrine, and by a holy city the Doctrine of Divine Truth; for Divine Truth is what is called holy in the WORD. That it is called the New Jerusalem is from a like reason that the earth is

called new: for, as was said just above, by earth is signified the Church, and by Jerusalem that church as to Doctrine. It is said to descend from GOD out of heaven, because all divine truth, from which is doctrine, descends out of heaven from the LORD. That by Jerusalem is not understood a city, although it was seen as a city, is clearly manifest from its being said that *its height was*, like the length and breadth, *twelve thousand furlongs*, vers. 16; and that *the measure of its wall, which was a hundred and forty-four cubits, was the measure of a man, that is, of an angel*, vers. 17; also, that it is said to be *prepared as a Bride adorned for her Husband*, vers. 2; and afterwards, "The angel said, Come, I will show thee the Bride, the LAMB'S Wife: and he showed me the Holy City, that Jerusalem," vers. 9, 10. The Church is what is called in the WORD the Bride and Wife of the LORD, — Bride before conjunction, and Wife when it is conjoined.

8. As regards the Doctrine in particular which now follows, it also is from heaven, because it is from the Spiritual Sense of the WORD; and the spiritual sense of the WORD is the same thing as the doctrine which is in heaven: for in heaven, equally as on the earth, there is a Church: for the WORD is there; doctrine from the WORD is there; temples are there, and in them are preachings performed: for there are governments there, ecclesiastical and civil: in a word, there arises no other difference between the things that are in the heavens and those which are on the earth, than that all things in the heavens are in a more perfect state, because all who are there are spiritual; and spiritual things immensely exceed natural ones in perfection. That there are such things in the heavens, may be seen

in the work on "Heaven and Hell" throughout; in particular in the chapter on Governments in Heaven, n. 213–220; and in the chapter on Divine Worship there, n. 221–227. From these things it may be evident, what is understood by the Holy City, New Jerusalem, being seen to descend from God out of heaven. But I proceed to the Doctrine itself, which is for the New Church; which, because it was revealed to me out of heaven, is called The Heavenly Doctrine: for to give this is the purpose of this work. H. D. 1–7. [See A. R. 876–960; T. C. R. 781–784.]

THE Nature and Design of the Lord's Second Coming; and the Origin of the New Church, signified by the New Jerusalem, which He has instituted; are also set forth as follows, in the "True Christian Religion, or Universal Theology" of that Church, given through the instrumentality of Emanuel Swedenborg, the servant of the Lord Jesus Christ:

FROM THE TRUE CHRISTIAN RELIGION, OR UNIVERSAL THEOLOGY, BY EMANUEL SWEDENBORG.

THE Consummation of the Age is the last Time or End of the Church. — On this earth there have been several churches; and all, in course of time, have been consummated: and after their consummation, new ones have existed; and thus even to the present time. The Consummation of a church takes place, when no divine truth remains except what is falsified or rejected: and when there is no genuine truth, no genuine good can be given; since all the quality of good is formed by truths: for, good is the essence of truth, and truth is the form of good; and without form, quality is not given. Good and truth can no more be separated, than the will and the understanding; or, what is the same, than the affection of love and the thought thence: wherefore, when the truth in the church is consummated, the good there is consummated also; and when this is done, then the church has an end; that is, it is the Consummation of it.

2. ON this earth, since its creation, there have been Four Churches in general, of which one has succeeded another; as may be evident from the WORD, both historical and prophetical: especially in Daniel, where those four churches are described by the statue of Nebuchadnezzar seen in a dream, (Dan. ii.,) and afterward by the four beasts coming up out of the sea, (vii.) The First Church, which is to be called the Most Ancient, existed before the flood, the Consummation or issue of which is described by the flood. The Second Church, which is to be called the Ancient, was in Asia, and partly in Africa; which was consummated and destroyed by idolatries. The Third Church was the Israelitish, begun by the promulgation of the Decalogue upon Mount Sinai, and continued by the WORD

written by Moses and the Prophets, and consummated or ended, by the profanation of the WORD, the fulness of which was at the time when the LORD came into the world: wherefore Him, who was the WORD, they crucified. The Fourth Church is the Christian, instituted by the LORD, through the Evangelists and the Apostles. Of this there have been two epochs; one from the time of the LORD to the Council of Nice, and the other from that council to the present day. But the latter in its progress has been divided into three parts, the Greek, the Roman Catholic, and the Reformed; but still, all these are called Christian. Besides, within each general church there have been several particular ones; which, although they have receded, have still retained the name from the general one, as the heresies in the Christian.

3. THE last time of the Christian Church is the very night into which the former churches have sunk down, as is evident from the LORD's prediction concerning it, in the Evangelists, and in Daniel. In the Evangelists, from these words: "That they should see the abomination of desolation; and that there should be great affliction, such as was not from the beginning of the world until now, nor shall be; and that unless those days should be shortened, no flesh could be saved; and finally, that the sun shall be darkened, and the moon shall not give her light, and the stars shall fall from the heaven." Matt. xxiv. 15, 21, 22, 29. That time is called night also elsewhere in the Evangelists, as in

Luke: "In that night there shall be two in one bed; one shall be taken, but the other shall be left." xvii. 34. And in John: "I must work the works of Him who sent ME; the night is coming, when no one will be able to work." ix. 4. Since all light departs at midnight, and the LORD is the true Light, (John i. 4, and the following verses: viii. 12; xii. 35, 36, 46,) therefore He said to the disciples, when He ascended into heaven: "I am with you even to the consummation of the age." Matt. xxviii. 20. And then He departs from them to a New Church. That this last time of the Church is the very night into which the former churches have sunk down, is evident also in Daniel, from these words: "At length, upon the bird of abominations shall be desolation, and even to the consummation and decision it shall drop upon the devastation." ix. 27. That this was foretold concerning the end of the Christian Church, is clearly manifest from the words of the LORD, Matt. xxiv. 15, and from many passages in the Prophets.

4. THAT Four Churches, since the creation of the world, have existed on this earth, is according to divine order; which is, that there should be a beginning, and an end of it, before a new beginning arises. Hence it is, that every day begins from Morning, and advances, and sinks down into Night, and after this begins anew; also that every year commences from Spring, and proceeds through Summer to Autumn, and ends in Winter, and after this begins again. It is for the effecting of

these things, that the Sun rises in the East, and proceeds thence through the South to the West, and sets in the North; from which it rises again. It is the like with the Churches: the First of them, which was the Most Ancient, was as the Morning, the Spring, and the East; the Second, or the Ancient, was as the Day, the Summer, and the South; the Third, as the Evening, the Autumn, and the West; and the Fourth, as the Night, the Winter, and the North. From these progressions according to order, the wise ancients concluded the four ages of the world; the first of which they called golden, the second silver, the third copper, and the fourth iron; with which metals also, the Churches themselves were represented in the image of Nebuchadnezzar.

5. THE Coming of the LORD is not His coming to destroy the visible heaven and the habitable earth, and to create a new heaven and a new earth, as many, hitherto, from not understanding the spiritual sense of the WORD, have thought. The opinion at this day prevailing in the churches is, that the LORD, when He shall come to the Last Judgment, will appear in the clouds of heaven, with angels, and the sound of trumpets; and will gather together all who dwell upon the earth, and also those who are deceased; and will separate the evil from the good, as a shepherd separates the goats from the sheep; and that then He will cast the evil, or the goats, into hell, and raise up the good, or the sheep, into heaven; and that then also He will create a new

visible heaven, and a new habitable earth; and upon the latter will send down a city, which will be called the New Jerusalem; the structure of which will be according to the description in Rev. xxi., namely, of jasper and gold; and the foundations of its wall, of every precious stone; and its height, breadth, and length, equal, each of twelve thousand furlongs; and that all the elect, both those who are living, and those that have died since the beginning of the world, will be gathered together into this city; and that they will then return into their bodies, and enjoy eternal bliss in that magnificent city, as in their heaven. This opinion concerning the Coming of the LORD, and concerning the Last Judgment, is at this day reigning in the Christian churches.

6. LEST, therefore, the man of the New Church, like the man of the old church, should wander in the shade in which the sense of the letter of the WORD is, especially concerning Heaven and Hell, and concerning his life after death, and here concerning the Coming of the LORD, it has pleased the LORD to open the sight of my spirit, and thus to let me into the Spiritual World; and not only to give me to speak with spirits and angels, and with relations and friends, but with kings and princes, who have departed from the natural world; and also to see the stupendous things of heaven, and the miserable things of hell; and thus that man does not stay after death in any limbo of the earth, nor fly about blind and dumb in the air or in empty space;

but that he lives as a man in a substantial body, in a much more perfect state, if he comes among the blessed, than before, when he lived in the material body. Therefore, lest man should plunge himself further into the opinion concerning the destruction of the visible heaven and the habitable earth, and thus concerning the spiritual world, from ignorance, which is the source of naturalism; and then at the same time atheism, which, at this day, among the learned, has begun to take root in the interior rational mind, should, like a mortification in the flesh, spread itself around more widely, even into his external mind, from which he speaks; it has been enjoined upon me by the LORD, to promulgate some of the things seen and heard, both concerning Heaven and Hell, and concerning the Last Judgment; and also to explain the Apocalypse, where the Coming of the LORD, and the former heaven, and the New Heaven, and the Holy Jerusalem, are treated of; from which, when read and understood, any one may see what is meant there by the Coming of the LORD, and by the New Heaven, and by the New Jerusalem.

7. THIS Coming of the LORD, which is the second, takes place in order that the evil may be separated from the good; and that those may be saved who have believed and do believe in HIM; and that a New Angelic Heaven may be formed from them, and a New Church on earth: and without it no flesh could be saved. Matt. xxiv. 22.—This Second Coming of the

LORD does not take place to destroy the visible heaven and the habitable earth, as has been shown in a foregoing paragraph. It is not to destroy anything, but to build up; consequently not to condemn, but to save, those who have believed in Him since His first coming, and who will hereafter believe; as is evident from these words of the LORD: "GOD sent not His SON into the world to judge the world, but that the world might be saved through Him. He that believeth in Him is not judged; but he that believeth not is already judged, because he hath not believed in the name of the only begotten SON of GOD." John iii. 17, 18. And again: "If any one hear My words, and yet believe not, I judge him not; for I came not to judge the world, but to save the world. He that despiseth Me, and receiveth not My words, hath that which judgeth him: the WORD which I have spoken, that will judge him." xii. 47, 48. The last judgment took place in the spiritual world in the year 1757, as has been shown in a little work concerning the "Last Judgment," published at London, in the year 1758; and further, in a "Continuation" concerning it, published at Amsterdam, 1763: which I testify, because I saw it with my eyes in full wakefulness.

8. THE Coming of the LORD is, to form a new heaven of those who have believed in Him, and to institute a New Church of those who hereafter believe in Him; because these two things are the ends of His coming. The very end of the creation of the universe

was no other than that an angelic heaven might be formed from men, in which all who believe in God are to live in eternal blessedness: for the Divine Love, which is in God, and essentially is God, cannot intend anything else; and the Divine Wisdom, which also is in God, and is God, can produce nothing else.

9. This second coming of the Lord is effected by means of a Man, before whom He has manifested Himself in person, and whom He has filled with His Spirit, to teach the doctrines of the New Church through the Word from Him. — Since the Lord cannot manifest Himself in person, as has been shown above (777), and yet He has foretold that He would come and establish a New Church, which is the New Jerusalem, it follows, that He is to do it by means of a man, who is able, not only to receive the Doctrines of this church with his understanding, but also to publish them by the press. That the Lord has manifested Himself before me, his servant, and sent me on this office, and that after this He opened the sight of my spirit, and thus let me into the spiritual world, and gave me to see the heavens and the hells, and also to speak with angels and spirits, and this now continually for many years, I testify in truth; likewise, that, from the first day of that call, I have not received anything that pertains to the doctrines of that church from any angel, but from the Lord alone while I read the Word.

10. To the end that the Lord might be constantly present, He has disclosed to me the Spiritual Sense of

His WORD, in which divine truth is in its light; and in this He is continually present: for His presence in the WORD is from no other ground than through the Spiritual Sense. Through the light of this He passes into the shade in which the sense of the letter is; comparatively as it happens with the light of the sun, in the daytime, by the interposition of a cloud. The sense of the letter of the WORD is as the cloud, and the spiritual sense is the glory; and the LORD Himself is the Sun from which the light proceeds: and thus the LORD is the WORD. The glory in which He is to come (Matt. xxiv. 30) signifies Divine Truth in its light, in which the spiritual sense of the WORD is.

11. THAT this New Church is to succeed the churches which have existed from the beginning of the world, and that it is to endure for ages of ages, and that thus it is to be the Crown of all the churches that have been before, was prophesied by Daniel; first, when he told and explained to Nebuchadnezzar his dream concerning the Four Kingdoms, by which are understood the Four Churches, represented by the statue seen by him, saying, "In the days of these, the GOD of the Heavens shall cause to arise a Kingdom, which shall not perish for ages; and it shall consume all those kingdoms, but it shall stand for ages," (Dan. ii. 44): and that this should be done by the STONE which became a great Rock, filling the whole earth, (35.) By a Rock, in the WORD, is understood the

Lord as to Divine Truth. And the same prophet elsewhere says, "I was seeing in the visions of the night, and behold, with the clouds of the heavens, as it were the Son of Man: and to Him was given dominion, and glory, and a kingdom; and all peoples, nations, and tongues shall worship Him. His dominion is the dominion of an age which will not pass away, and His kingdom one which will not perish," (vii. 13, 14.) And this he says after he saw the four beasts coming up out of the sea, (verse 3); by which also the four former churches were represented. That these things were prophesied by Daniel concerning this time, is evident from his words, chap. xii. 4; and also from the words of the Lord, Matt. xxiv. 15, 30. The like is said in the Revelation: "The seventh angel sounded: then there came great voices out of heaven, saying, 'The kingdoms of the world are become our Lord's and His Christ's; and He shall reign for ages of ages.'" xi. 15.

12. What this Church is to be, is described at large in the Revelation, where the end of the former church, and the rise of the New, are treated of. This New Church is described by the New Jerusalem, and by its magnificent things; and that it is to be the Bride and Wife of the Lamb. xix. 7; xxi. 2, 9. Besides, I will take from the Revelation only these words: When the New Jerusalem was seen to descend out of heaven, it is said, "Behold, the tabernacle of God is with men, and He will dwell with them, and

they shall be His people, and He will be with them, their God: And the nations that are saved shall walk in the light of it; and night shall not be there. I, Jesus, have sent My angel to testify to you these things in the Churches. I am the Root and the Offspring of David, the bright and the morning Star. And the Spirit and the Bride say, Come; and let him that heareth say, Come; and let him that thirsteth come; and he that will, let him take water of life freely. Yea, Come, Lord Jesus: Amen." xxi. 3, 24, 25; xxii. 16, 17, 20.—T. C. R. 753, 760, 761, 762, 768, 771, 772, 773, 779, 780, 788, 790.

[See A. R. 194, 330, 532–565, 876–960; A. E. 223, 280, 433, 629, 717; T. C. R. 781–784; A. C. 1850, 3353–3356, 3486–3489, 3650–3655, 3751–3757, 3897–3901, 4056–4060, 4229–4231, 4332–4335, 4422–4424, 4535, 4635–4638; L. J. 70; C. L. J. 10.]

PART II.

DOCTRINES OF THE NEW CHURCH.

PART II.

DOCTRINES OF THE NEW CHURCH.

INTRODUCTION TO THE DOCTRINE.

FROM THE NEW JERUSALEM AND ITS HEAVENLY DOCTRINE, BY EMANUEL SWEDENBORG.

THAT there is an end to the church when there is no faith because there is no charity, was shown in the small work on the "Last Judgment and the Destruction of Babylon," n. 33–39, and further. Now since the churches in the Christian world had distinguished themselves only by such things as are of faith, — and still there is no faith where there is no charity, — therefore I wish to premise here, before the Doctrine itself, some things concerning the Doctrine of Charity with the Ancients. It is said, *the churches in the Christian world;* and by them are understood the churches with the Reformed or Evangelical, but not with the Papists; since the Christian church is not there: for, where the church is, there the LORD is adored, and the WORD is read. With them it is otherwise: there themselves are adored instead of the LORD, and the WORD is forbidden to be read by the people; and the *dictum* of the pope is put equal to it; yea, above it.

2. THE Doctrine of Charity, which is the doctrine

of life, was doctrine itself in the Ancient Churches; and that doctrine conjoined all churches, and so out of many made one: for, all those who lived in the good of charity they acknowledged as men of the church, and called them brethren, howsoever they might differ besides in the truths which at this day are called truths of faith. In these one instructed another, — which was among their works of charity: nor were they also offended, if one did not accede to another's opinion; knowing that every one receives so much of truth as he is in good. Since the ancient churches were such, they were therefore more internal men; and because more internal, they were wiser: for they who are in the good of love and charity are in heaven as to the internal man, and as to the same are in an angelic society there which is in like good. Thence there is an elevation of their mind to interior things; and consequently they have wisdom. For wisdom can come from nowhere else but from heaven, that is, through heaven from the LORD; and in heaven there is wisdom, because there they are in good. Wisdom is to see truth from the light of truth; and the light of truth is the light which is in heaven. But that ancient wisdom in process of time decreased: for, as far as the human race removed itself from the good of love to the LORD and love towards the neighbor, which love is called Charity, so far it removed itself also from wisdom, because so far from heaven. Hence it is, that man from internal became external, and this gradually. And when man became external, he also became worldly and corporeal; and when he is such, he cares little for the things that are of heaven. For the delights of earthly loves then occupy him wholly, and with them the evils which are delightful to man from those loves: and then the things which he hears concerning the life after death, concerning heaven and hell, in a word, concerning spiritual things, are as if out of him, and not within him; as they nevertheless ought to be. Hence also it is, that the Doctrine of Charity, which had been so highly valued with the ancients, is at this day among the things that are lost: for, who at this day knows what charity in the genuine sense is? and what in the genuine sense the neighbor is? when yet that doctrine not only teaches it, but innumerable things besides; not the thousandth part of which is known at this day. The whole Sacred Scripture is nothing else but the Doctrine of Love and Charity; which the LORD also teaches, saying, "Thou shalt love the LORD thy GOD from thy whole heart, and in thy whole soul, and in thy whole mind: this is the First and Great Commandment. The Second is like to it: Thou shalt love thy neighbor as thyself. On these two Commandments hang all the Law and the Prophets." Matt. xxii. 37–40. The Law and the Prophets, in each and every thing of them, are the WORD. H. D. 8, 9.

[See A. C. 809, 904, 1121, 1285, 1316, 1515, 1798, 1799, 1834, 1844, 2385, 2417, 2425, 2454, 2545, 2982, 3321, 3419, 3445, 6627–6633, 7085, 7258, 7263, 10,763, 10,765.]

CHAPTER I.

CONCERNING THE LORD, THE DIVINE TRINITY, AND REDEMPTION.

Hear, O Israel; the LORD our GOD is ONE LORD. Deut. vi. 4; Mark xii. 29.

There is ONE GOD, and there is none other but HE. Mark xii. 32.

Unto us a CHILD is born, unto us a SON is given: and His name shall be called Wonderful, Counsellor, GOD, Mighty, the EVERLASTING FATHER, the Prince of Peace. Isa. ix. 6.

I and the FATHER are ONE. John x. 30.

FROM THE NEW JERUSALEM AND ITS HEAVENLY DOCTRINE, BY EMANUEL SWEDENBORG.

THERE is one GOD, who is the Creator of the universe and the Preserver of the universe; thus who is the GOD of heaven and the GOD of the earth.

2. THERE are two things which make the life of heaven with man, the good of love and the truth of faith. This life man has from GOD, and nothing at all from man; on which account the primary thing of

the church is, to acknowledge GOD, to believe in GOD, and to love Him.

3. THEY who are born within the Church ought to acknowledge the LORD, His Divinity and His Humanity, and to believe in Him, and to love Him; for from the LORD is all salvation. This the LORD teaches in John: "He that believeth on the SON, hath eternal life: but he that believeth not the SON, shall not see life; but the anger of GOD remaineth with him." iii. 36. In the same: "This is the will of Him that sent ME, that every one that seeth the SON, and believeth on Him, should have eternal life; and I will raise him up in the last day." vi. 40. In the same: "JESUS said, I am the resurrection and the life: he that believeth in ME, though he die, shall live; and every one that liveth and believeth in ME, shall never die." xi. 25, 26.

4. WHEREFORE they within the church, who do not acknowledge the LORD and His Divinity, cannot be conjoined to GOD, nor thus have any lot with the angels in heaven: for no one can be conjoined to GOD, except from the LORD and in the LORD. That no one can be conjoined to GOD except *from* the LORD, the LORD teaches in John: "No one hath ever seen GOD: the only begotten SON, who is in the bosom of the FATHER, He hath brought Him forth." i. 18. In the same: "Ye have never heard His voice, nor seen His shape." v. 37. In Matthew: "No one knoweth the FATHER but the SON, and he to whom

the SON willeth to reveal Him." xi. 27. And in John: "I am the Way, the Truth, and the Life: no one cometh to the FATHER, but by ME." xiv. 6. That no one can be conjoined to GOD except *in* the LORD, is because the FATHER is in Him, and they are ONE; as He also teaches in John: "If ye know ME, ye know My FATHER also: he that seeth ME, seeth the FATHER: Philip, believest thou not that I am in the FATHER, and the FATHER in ME? believe ME, that I am in the FATHER, and the FATHER in ME." xiv. 7–11. And in the same: "The FATHER and I are ONE. That ye may know, and believe, that I am in the FATHER, and the FATHER in ME." x. 30, 38.

5. SINCE the FATHER is in the LORD, and the FATHER and the LORD are ONE; and since we must believe in Him, and he that believeth in Him hath eternal life; it is manifest that the LORD is GOD. That the LORD is GOD the WORD teaches, as in John: "In the beginning was the WORD, and the WORD was with GOD, and GOD WAS THE WORD. All things were made by Him, and without Him was nothing made that was made. And the WORD WAS MADE FLESH, and dwelt among us; and we beheld His glory, the glory as of the ONLY-BEGOTTEN of the FATHER." i. 1, 3, 14. In Isaiah: "A CHILD is born to us, a SON is given to us; upon whose shoulder shall be the sovereignty; and His name shall be called GOD, Hero, FATHER OF ETERNITY, Prince of Peace." ix. 6. In the same: "A virgin shall conceive

and bring forth, and shall call His name GOD WITH US." vii. 14; Matt. i. 23. And in Jeremiah: "Behold, the days shall come, when I will raise up to David a righteous BRANCH, who shall reign KING, and shall prosper: and this is His name that they shall call Him, JEHOVAH OUR RIGHTEOUSNESS." xxiii. 5, 6; xxxiii. 15, 16.

6. ALL who are of the Church, and in light from Heaven, see the Divinity in the LORD; but they that are not in light from heaven, see nothing but the Humanity in the LORD: when yet the Divinity and the Humanity are so united in Him, that they are one; as the LORD also teaches elsewhere in John: "FATHER, all MINE are THINE, and all THINE are MINE." xvii. 10.

7. THAT the LORD was conceived of JEHOVAH the FATHER, and is thus GOD by conception, is known in the church: and also that He rose with the whole body; for He left nothing in the sepulchre: concerning which also He afterwards confirmed the disciples, saying, "Behold My hands and My feet, that it is I MYSELF: handle ME and see; for a spirit hath not flesh and bones, as ye see ME have." Luke xxiv. 39. And though He was a man as to flesh and bones, still He entered through closed doors; and after He had manifested Himself, became invisible. John xx. 19, 26; Luke xxiv. 3. It is otherwise with every man; for man rises only as to the spirit, and not as to the body: wherefore, when He said *that He was not*

like a spirit, He said that He was not like another man. Hence it is manifest that the Humanity also in the Lord is Divine.

8. Every man has his *esse* of life, which is called his soul, from his father; the *existere* of life thence is what is called the body: hence the body is the effigy of its soul; for through it the soul acts its life at will. Hence it is, that men are born into the likeness of their parents, and that families are known apart. It is hence manifest what kind of body, or what a Humanity, the Lord had; namely, that it was as the Divinity Itself, which was the *esse* of His life, or His soul, from the Father: wherefore He said, "He that seeth Me, seeth the Father." John xiv. 9.

9. That the Divinity and the Humanity of the Lord are one person, is according to the Faith received in the whole Christian world, which is this: "Although Christ is God and Man, still He is not two, but one Christ; yea, He is altogether one, and a single person: since as the body and soul are one man, so also God and Man is one Christ." This is from the Creed of Athanasius.

10. They who have concerning the Divinity an idea of three persons, cannot have the idea of One God: if with the mouth they say one, still they think three. But they who concerning the Divinity have the idea of three in one person, can have an idea of One God, and can say One God, and also think One God.

11. The idea of three in one person is had, when it

is thought that the FATHER is in the LORD, and that the HOLY SPIRIT proceeds from Him. Then there is a Trine in the LORD, — the Divinity Itself which is called the FATHER, the Divine Humanity which is the SON, and the Divine Proceeding which is the HOLY SPIRIT.

12. SINCE in the LORD all is Divine, therefore He has all power in heaven and in earth; which He also says in John: "The FATHER hath given all things into the hand of the SON." iii. 35. In the same: "The FATHER hath given to the SON power over all flesh." xvii. 2. In Matthew: "All things are delivered unto ME of My FATHER." xi. 27. In the same: "All power is given unto ME in heaven and in earth." xxviii. 18. Such power is DIVINITY.

13. THEY who make the LORD's Humanity like to the humanity of another man, do not think of His conception from the Divinity Itself; nor do they consider that the body of every one is the effigy of his soul: neither do they think of His resurrection with His whole body; nor of Him as seen when He was transfigured, that His face shone as the sun: nor do they think of those things which the LORD said concerning faith in Him, concerning His oneness with the FATHER, concerning His glorification, and concerning His power over heaven and earth, — that these are divine things, and are said of His Humanity. Nor do they recollect that the LORD is omnipresent also as to His Humanity; (Matt. xxviii. 20;) yet thence is the belief of His om-

nipresence in the Holy Supper: Omnipresence is Divine. Yea, perhaps they do not think that the Divine which is called the HOLY SPIRIT proceeds from His Humanity; when yet it proceeds from His glorified Humanity: for it is said, "The HOLY SPIRIT was not yet, because JESUS was not yet glorified." John vii. 39.

14. THE LORD came into the world, that He might save the human race, which otherwise would have perished by eternal death: and He did save them by this, that He subjugated the hells, which infested every man coming into the world and going out of the world; and at the same time by His glorifying His Humanity: for thus He can hold the hells subjugated forever. The subjugation of the hells, and at the same time the glorification of His Humanity, were effected by temptations admitted into the Humanity which He had from the mother, and by continual victories then. His passion on the cross was the last temptation, and full victory.

15. THAT the LORD subjugated the hells, He teaches in John: when the passion of the cross was at hand, then JESUS said, "Now is the Judgment of this world, NOW SHALL THE PRINCE OF THIS WORLD BE CAST OUT." xii. 31. In the same: "Trust ye; I HAVE OVERCOME THE WORLD." xvi. 33. And in Isaiah: "Who is this that cometh from Edom, walking in the greatness of His strength, mighty to save: My arm brought salvation to ME; therefore He became a

SAVIOR to them." lxiii. 1–19; lix. 16–21. That He glorified His Humanity, and that the passion of the cross was the last temptation and full victory, by which He was glorified, He also teaches in John: "After Judas went out, JESUS said, Now is the SON OF MAN glorified, and GOD will glorify Him in Himself, and will straightway glorify Him." xiii. 31, 32. In the same: "FATHER, the hour is come; glorify Thy SON, that Thy SON also may glorify Thee." xvii. 1, 5. In the same: "Now is My soul troubled; FATHER, glorify Thy Name: and there came forth a voice from heaven, I have both glorified, and will glorify again." xii. 27, 28. And in Luke: "Was it not necessary for CHRIST to suffer these things, and to enter into glory?" xxiv. 26. These things were said of His passion: to glorify is to make Divine. Hence now it is evident, that unless the LORD came into the world, and became Man, and in that way liberated from hell all those that believe in Him, and love Him, no mortal could be saved. Thus is it understood, that without the LORD there is no salvation.

16. WHEN the LORD fully glorified His Humanity, He then put off the Humanity from the mother, and put on the Humanity from the FATHER, which is the DIVINE HUMANITY; wherefore He was then no longer the son of Mary.

17. THE first and primary thing of the Church is, to know and acknowledge its GOD: for without that knowledge and acknowledgment there is no conjunc-

tion, — thus, in the Church, without the acknowledgment of the LORD. This the LORD teaches in John: "He that believeth on the SON, hath eternal life: but he that believeth not the SON, shall not see life; but the anger of GOD remaineth with him." iii. 36. And elsewhere: "Unless ye believe that I am, ye shall die in your sins." viii. 24.

18. THAT there is a Trine in the LORD, namely, the DIVINITY, the DIVINE HUMANITY, and the DIVINE PROCEEDING, is an arcanum from heaven; and it is for those who will be in the Holy Jerusalem. H. D. 280–297.

[See D. L. 1–65; T. C. R. 81–137, 163–188; A. C. 14, 15, 23, 128, 129, 223, 1414, 1432, 1438, 1444, 1460, 1461, 1554, 1557, 1573, 1602, 1603, 1607, 1616, 1659, 1661, 1663, 1673, 1676, 1690, 1692, 1707, 1725, 1729, 1735, 1736, 1745, 1785–1787, 1799, 1813, 1815, 1864, 1904, 1914, 1919, 1921, 1950, 1999, 2004, 2005, 2010, 2016, 2021, 2025, 2034, 2059, 2093, 2149, 2156, 2288, 2343, 2658, 2663, 2816, 2841, 2921, 3023, 3035, 3038, 3061–3063, 3704, 3737, 3969, 4319, 4417, 4641, 4692, 4727, 5110, 5256, 5663, 6303, 6685, 6834, 6849, 6993, 7444, 8864, 9194, 9276, 9303, 9315, 9937, 10,152, 10,154, 10,196; A. E. 151, 178, 328, 460; A. R. 341, 743, 829, 933, 962.]

CHAPTER II.

CONCERNING THE WORD.

IN THE BEGINNING was the WORD, and the WORD was with GOD, and the WORD was GOD. John i. 1.

For ever, O JEHOVAH, Thy WORD is established IN THE HEAVENS. Ps. cxix. 89.

JEHOVAH gave the WORD. Ps. lxviii. 11.

The WORDS that I speak unto you are SPIRIT and are LIFE. John vi. 63.

FROM THE NEW JERUSALEM AND ITS HEAVENLY DOCTRINE, BY EMANUEL SWEDENBORG.

MAN, without a Revelation from the Divine, cannot know anything concerning eternal life, nor indeed anything concerning GOD, and still less concerning love to and faith in Him. For man is born into mere ignorance; and then from worldly things he must learn all the things from which he will form his understanding. He is also born hereditarily into all evil, which is from the love of self and of the world. The delights therefrom reign continually, and suggest such things as are diametrically against the Divine. Hence then it is, that man knows nothing of eternal life: consequently there must necessarily be a Revelation, from which he may know.

2. THAT the evils of the love of self and the world induce such ignorance of the things which are of eternal life, is plainly manifest from those within the church, who — although they know from revelation that there is a GOD, that there are a heaven and a hell, that there is eternal life, and that that life is to be procured by good of life and of faith — still fall into the denial of them, as well the learned as the unlearned. Hence again it is manifest, how great ignorance there would be, if there were no Revelation.

3. SINCE, therefore, man lives after death, and then to eternity, and a life awaits him according to his love and faith, it follows that the Divine has, from love towards the human race, revealed such things as lead to that life, and conduce to his salvation. What the Divine has revealed is with us the WORD.

4. THE WORD, because it is a revelation from the Divine, is divine in each and every thing; for what is from the Divine cannot be otherwise. That which is from the Divine, descends through the Heavens even to man: on which account, in the heavens it is accommodated to the wisdom of the angels who are there, and on the earth it is accommodated to the comprehension of men who are there. Wherefore in the WORD there is an internal sense, which is spiritual, for the angels; and an external sense, which is natural, for men.

Hence it is, that there is a conjunction of heaven with man through the WORD.

5. THE genuine sense of the WORD no others understand but they who are illustrated; and they only are illustrated, who are in love to and faith in the LORD: for their interiors are elevated by the LORD into the light of heaven.

6. THE WORD in the letter cannot be comprehended, except by Doctrine drawn from the WORD by one who is illustrated. The sense of its letter is accommodated to the comprehension of men, however simple; wherefore Doctrine from the WORD must be to them for a lantern.

FROM THE HEAVENLY ARCANA, BY EMANUEL SWEDENBORG.

7. THE Books of the WORD are all those which have the Internal Sense: but those which have it not, are not the WORD. The Books of the WORD, in the Old Testament, are the five books of Moses, the book of Joshua, the book of Judges, the two books of Samuel, the two books of the Kings, the Psalms of David; the Prophets, Isaiah, Jeremiah, Lamentations, Ezekiel, Daniel, Hosea, Joel, Amos, Obadiah, Jonah, Micah, Nahum, Habakkuk, Zephaniah, Haggai, Zechariah, Malachi: and in the New Testament, the four Evangelists, Matthew, Mark, Luke, John; and the Apocalypse.* A. C. 10,325.

* The other Books of the BIBLE are in a style different from the Divine style of the WORD; not being dictated to the writers immediately by the LORD Himself as His "WORD." They

have in them no internal sense, in a connected series from the LORD; though some of them are written in a degree according to Correspondences.

While the Books of the WORD have an immediate communication with the LORD and with Heaven, by means of their Spiritual Sense, the Apostolical Writings, being merely doctrinal, and having all their meaning in the literal sense, communicate only mediately or indirectly with Heaven. Hence they are very good Books of the Church, insisting on the doctrines of love and faith taught by the LORD in the Gospels and in the Book of Revelation.

[See S. S. 1–118; W. H. 1–17; T. C. R. 189–335, 846; A. C. 64–66, 167, 571, 582, 589, 605, 755, 920, 937, 1143, 1405, 1408, 1409, 1502, 1540, 1659, 1756, 1767–1777, 1783, 1807, 1869–1879, 1886–1888, 1929, 1965, 1984, 2015, 2135, 2143, 2179, 2212, 2242, 2310, 2333, 2362, 2495, 2520, 2523, 2533, 2553, 2592, 2593, 2606–2609, 2686, 2712, 2760, 2763, 2894–2900, 4807, 4816, 4857, 4989, 5648, 5702, 6333, 6343, 6516, 6597, 6789, 7153, 7381, 7933, 8106, 8615, 8682, 8694, 8783, 8862, 8943, 8944, 9211, 9212, 9280, 9349–9362, 9407, 9942, 10,355, 10,400, 10,632–10,634; A. E. 17, 176, 208, 238, 365, 376, 382, 408, 484, 593, 734, 816, 832, 916, 1024, 1065, 1066, 1074, 1076, 1077, 1080, 1083; H. H. 87–115, 303–310.]

CHAPTER III.

CONCERNING THE THEOLOGICAL WRITINGS OF EMANUEL SWEDENBORG.

These things have I spoken unto you in PROVERBS: but the time cometh when I shall no more speak unto you in PROVERBS; but I shall SHOW YOU PLAINLY of the FATHER. John xvi. 25.

The SON OF MAN shall come in the CLOUDS OF HEAVEN with GREAT POWER AND GLORY. Matt. xxiv. 30.

The Woman clothed with the Sun brought forth a MAN CHILD, who is to act the shepherd over all nations with a CROOK OF IRON. Rev. xii. 1, 5.

THE Theological Writings of Emanuel Swedenborg do not, like the WORD, contain an internal or spiritual sense. They were, nevertheless, written by Divine "command," contain "truths continuous from the LORD," and hence are to be received as divinely authorized expositions of the Sacred Scriptures, and of the laws of Divine Order concerning the Church.

FROM THE TRUE CHRISTIAN RELIGION, BY EMANUEL SWEDENBORG.

SINCE the LORD cannot manifest Himself in person, as has been shown just above, (T. C. R. 777,) and yet He has foretold that He would come, and establish a New Church, which is the New Jerusalem, it follows that He is to do it by means of a man, who is able not only to receive the Doctrines of this Church with his understanding, but also to publish them by the press. That the LORD manifested Himself before me, His servant, and sent me on this office, and that after this He opened the sight of my spirit, and thus let me into the spiritual world, and gave me to see the heavens and the hells, and also to speak with angels and spirits, and this now for many years, I testify in truth; likewise that, from the first day of that call, I have not received anything that pertains to the Doctrines of that Church from any angel, but from the LORD alone while I read the WORD.

2. To the end that the LORD might be constantly present, He has disclosed to me the spiritual sense of His WORD, in which divine truth is in its light; and in this He is continually present.

3. THE Doctrines of the New Church are truths continuous from the LORD, laid open through the WORD. T. C. R. 779, 780, 508.

FROM THE NEW JERUSALEM AND ITS HEAVENLY DOCTRINE, BY EMANUEL SWEDENBORG.

4. AND the Doctrine is called THE HEAVENLY DOCTRINE, because it was revealed to me out of Heaven; for to give this Doctrine is the purpose of this work. H. D. 7.

FROM THE TRUE CHRISTIAN RELIGION, BY EMANUEL SWEDENBORG.

5. SINCE it has been given me by the LORD to see the wonderful things which are in the heavens and under the heavens, it behooves me, according to command, to relate what has been seen.

6. LEST, therefore, the man of the New Church, like the man of the old church, should wander in the shade in which the sense of the letter of the WORD is, especially concerning heaven and hell, and concerning his life after death, and here concerning the Coming of the LORD, it has pleased the LORD to open the eyes of my spirit, and thus to let me into the spiritual world. * * * * It has been *enjoined upon me by the* LORD, *to promulgate some of the things seen and heard.*

7. I FORESEE that many who read the Relations after the chapters, will believe that they are inventions of the imagination; but I assert in truth, that they are not inventions, but were truly seen and heard: not seen and heard in any state of the mind asleep, but in a state of full wakefulness. For it has pleased the LORD to manifest Himself to me, and to send me to teach those things which will be of His

New Church, which is understood by the New Jerusalem in the Revelation. T. C. R. 188, 771, 851.

CATALOGUE OF THE THEOLOGICAL WRITINGS OF EMANUEL SWEDENBORG, WITH THE DATES OF THEIR PUBLICATION.

THE HEAVENLY ARCANA (Arcana Cœlestia), which are in the Sacred Scripture or Word of the Lord, laid open: Genesis and Exodus: together with the wonders which were seen in the World of Spirits and in the Heaven of the Angels. 12 vols. octavo. 1749–1756.

CONCERNING THE NEW JERUSALEM AND ITS HEAVENLY DOCTRINE, from things heard out of Heaven: to which is prefixed something concerning the New Heaven and New Earth. 1758.

CONCERNING THE LAST JUDGMENT AND THE DESTRUCTION OF BABYLON; showing that all the things which are foretold in the Apocalypse are at this day fulfilled: From things heard and seen. 1758.

CONCERNING HEAVEN AND ITS WONDERS, AND CONCERNING HELL: From things heard and seen. 1758.

CONCERNING THE EARTHS IN OUR SOLAR SYSTEM, which are called Planets; and concerning Earths in the Starry Heaven; and concerning their inhabitants: also, concerning the Spirits and Angels there: From things heard and seen. 1758.

CONCERNING THE WHITE HORSE, mentioned in the Apocalypse, chap. xix.; and also concerning the Word and its Spiritual or Internal Sense, from the Heavenly Arcana. 1758.

A CONTINUATION CONCERNING THE LAST JUDGMENT, and concerning the Spiritual World. 1763.

THE DOCTRINE OF THE NEW JERUSALEM CONCERNING THE LORD. 1763.

THE DOCTRINE OF THE NEW JERUSALEM CONCERNING THE SACRED SCRIPTURE. 1763.

THE DOCTRINE OF LIFE FOR THE NEW JERUSALEM, from the Precepts of the Decalogue. 1763.

THE DOCTRINE OF THE NEW JERUSALEM CONCERNING FAITH. 1763.

THE ANGELIC WISDOM CONCERNING THE DIVINE LOVE AND THE DIVINE WISDOM. 1763.

THE ANGELIC WISDOM CONCERNING THE DIVINE PROVIDENCE. 1764.

THE APOCALYPSE REVEALED; in which are laid open the Arcana which are there foretold, and have hitherto lain concealed. 2 vols. octavo. 1766.

THE DELIGHTS OF WISDOM CONCERNING CONJUGIAL LOVE;— After which follow the Pleasures of Insanity concerning Scortatory Love. 1768.

ON THE INTERCOURSE BETWEEN THE SOUL AND THE BODY; which is believed to take place either by Physical Influx, or by Spiritual Influx, or by Preëstablished Harmony. 1769.

A BRIEF EXPOSITION OF THE DOCTRINE OF THE NEW CHURCH, which is understood by the New Jerusalem in the Apocalypse. 1769.

THE TRUE CHRISTIAN RELIGION, containing the UNIVERSAL THEOLOGY of the New Church, foretold by the Lord in Daniel vii. 13, 14; and in the Apocalypse xxi. 1, 2. 1771.

The following were published from his manuscripts after his death:—

THE APOCALYPSE EXPLAINED ACCORDING TO THE SPIRITUAL SENSE; wherein are revealed the Arcana which are there foretold, and have hitherto been concealed. 6 vols. octavo. Written 1759–1762.

A CORONIS OR APPENDIX TO THE TRUE CHRIS-

TIAN RELIGION; treating of the Four Churches on this Earth since the Creation of the World, and of their Periods and Consummation; and further, of the New Church which is to succeed those Four, which will be truly Christian, and the Crown of the preceding: Also, of the Coming of the Lord to it, and of His Divine Auspices in it to eternity; and besides, of the Mystery of Redemption. Unfinished.

THE DOCTRINE OF THE NEW JERUSALEM CONCERNING CHARITY. Unfinished.

THE CANONS OF THE ENTIRE THEOLOGY OF THE NEW CHURCH: concerning the One and Infinite God; concerning the Lord the Redeemer, and concerning Redemption; concerning the Holy Spirit; and concerning the Divine Trinity. Unfinished.

A SUMMARY EXPOSITION OF THE INTERNAL SENSE of the Prophetic Books of the Word of the Old Testament, and also of the Psalms of David; with a two-fold Index.

[See T. C. R. 192–194, 200, 508, 776–782, 846–851; A. C. 1–5, 64–72, 166, 167, preface to Genesis xvi.; C. L. 1, 26; H. H. 1; E. U. 1, 123–127.]

CHAPTER IV.

CONCERNING DIVINE PROVIDENCE.

Not a sparrow shall fall upon the earth without your FATHER. And the hairs of your head also are all numbered. Matt. x. 29, 30.

THE LORD'S Government in the heavens and on the earth is called Providence: and since every good which is of love and every truth which is of faith, from which is salvation, is from Him, and nothing at all from man, it is hence manifest, that the LORD'S Divine Providence is in all and each of the things that conduce to the salvation of the human race. This the LORD thus teaches in John: "I am the Way, the Truth, and the Life," xiv. 6; and again: "As the branch cannot bear fruit of itself, unless it abide in the vine; so neither ye, unless ye abide in ME: without ME ye can do nothing." xv. 4, 5.

2. THE LORD'S Divine Providence is over the most minute things of man's life: for there is but one only Fountain of life, which is the LORD; from whom we are, live, and act.

3. THEY who think of the Divine Providence from worldly things, conclude from them that it is only universal; and that the particulars are left to man. But they do not know the arcana of heaven; for they conclude only from the loves of self and the world, and from the pleasures of them. Wherefore, when they see the evil raised to honors and gaining wealth more than the good, and also succeeding according to their arts, they say in their heart, that it would not be so, if there were a Divine Providence in each and every thing. But they do not consider that the Divine Providence does not regard that which quickly passes away, and has its end with man's life in the world; but that it regards that which remains forever, thus that which has no end. That which has no end, Is; but what has an end, that in comparison Is not. Let one think, if he can, whether a hundred thousand years are anything to eternity; and he will perceive that they are not. What then are a few years of life in the world?

4. HE who rightly weighs, may know that eminence and opulence in the world are not real divine blessings, though man from his lust calls them so; for they pass away, and also seduce many, and turn them away from heaven: but that eternal life and its happiness are the real blessings, which are from the Divine. This the LORD also teaches in Luke: "Make to yourselves a treasure in the heavens that faileth not; where the thief cometh not, nor the moth corrupteth: for where

your treasure is, there will your heart be also." xii. 33, 34.

5. THAT the evil succeed according to their arts, is from the cause that it is according to Divine Order that every one should act what he acts from Reason and also from Freedom; on which account, unless it were left to man to act from freedom according to his reason, and unless also the acts which are thence should thus succeed, man could in no way be disposed to receiving eternal life; for this is insinuated when man is in freedom and his reason is enlightened. For no one can be forced to good; since everything forced does not inhere: for it is not his. That becomes man's own which is done from freedom according to his reason; and that is done from freedom, which is done from the will or love: and the will or love is the man himself. If man were forced to that which he does not will, he would still incline in mind to that which he does will: and besides, every one strives after what is forbidden, and this from the latent cause that it is after freedom. Hence it is manifest, that unless man were kept in freedom, good could not be provided for him.

6. To leave man also from his freedom to think, to will, and, as far as the laws do not prohibit, to do, evil, is called permitting.

7. To be led to happy things in the world by arts, appears to man as if it were from his own prudence; but still the Divine Providence perpetually accompanies, by permitting, and continually withdrawing from

evil. But to be led to happy things in heaven, is known and perceived not to be from one's own prudence, because from the LORD; and it is done of His Divine Providence, by disposing, and continually leading to good.

8. THAT it is so, man cannot comprehend from the light of nature; for from that he knows not the Laws of Divine Order.

9. IT is to be known, that there is Providence and Foresight. Good is what is provided by the LORD, but evil is what is foreseen by the LORD. The one must be with the other: for what comes from man is nothing but evil; but what is from the LORD is nothing but good. H. D. 267–275.

[See the work on Divine Providence entire: also, A. C. 1919, 2694, 3854, 5122, 5155, 5195, 5264, 5508, 6480–6495, 6574, 7004, 7007, 8478, 8480, 8717, 9128, 10,409; A. E. 1136, 1138, 1139, 1141–1148, 1150–1156, 1158–1160, 1162–1168, 1170, 1171, 1173–1177, 1179, 1180, 1182, 1183, 1185–1191.]

CHAPTER V.

CONCERNING GOOD AND TRUTH.

O JEHOVAH, who shall sojourn in thy tabernacle? who shall dwell in the mountain of thy holiness? He that speaketh the TRUTH in his HEART. Ps. xv. 1, 2.

GRACE and TRUTH came by JESUS CHRIST. John i. 17.

FROM THE NEW JERUSALEM AND ITS HEAVENLY DOCTRINE, BY EMANUEL SWEDENBORG.

ALL things in the universe, which are according to Divine Order, refer themselves to GOOD and TRUTH. Nothing exists in heaven, and nothing in the world, which does not refer itself to these two. The reason is, that each, as well Good as Truth, proceeds from the Divine, from whom all things are.

2. IT is hence manifest, that nothing is more necessary to man than to know what good is and what truth is; also how the one regards the other, and how the one is conjoined to the other. But it is the most necessary to the man of the Church: for, as all things of Heaven refer themselves to good and truth, so also

do all things of the Church; since the good and truth of heaven are also the good and truth of the church. This is the reason that the commencement is made with Good and Truth.

3. It is according to Divine Order, that good and truth should be conjoined, and not separated; thus that they should be one, and not two: for they proceed conjoined from the Divine; and they are conjoined in Heaven: therefore also they must be conjoined in the Church. The conjunction of good and truth is called in heaven the Heavenly Marriage; for in this marriage are all who are there. Hence it is, that in the Word heaven is compared to a marriage; and that the Lord is called the Bridegroom and Husband, but Heaven the Bride and Wife: and the Church the same. Heaven and the Church are so called, because they who are therein receive divine good in truths.

4. All the intelligence and wisdom which the angels have are from that marriage, and not any from good separate from truth, nor from truth separate from good. It is the same with the men of the Church.

5. Since the conjunction of good and truth is like a marriage, it is manifest that good loves truth, and that in return truth loves good; and that the one desires to be conjoined with the other. The man of the Church who has not such love and such desire, is not in the Heavenly Marriage; thus the church is not as yet in him: for the conjunction of good and truth makes the church.

6. GOODS are manifold: in general there is spiritual good and natural good; and both are conjoined in genuine moral good. As goods are manifold, so also are truths; since truths are of good, and are the forms of good.

7. As it is with good and truth, so it is by opposition with evil and falsity: namely, that as all things in the universe which are according to divine order refer themselves to good and truth, so all things which are contrary to divine order refer themselves to evil and falsity: also, that as good loves to be conjoined to truth, and truth to good; so evil loves to be conjoined to falsity, and falsity to evil: as also, since all intelligence and wisdom are born from the conjunction of good and truth, so are all insanity and folly from the conjunction of evil and falsity. The conjunction of evil and falsity is called the infernal marriage.

8. FROM the fact that evil and falsity are opposite to good and truth, it is manifest that truth cannot be conjoined to evil, nor good to the falsity of evil. If truth is adjoined to evil, it becomes no longer truth, but falsity; because it is falsified: and if good is adjoined to the falsity of evil, it becomes no longer good, but evil; because it is adulterated. But falsity which is not of evil can be conjoined to good.

9. NO one who is in evil and thence in falsity from confirmation and life, can know what good and truth are; since he believes his evil to be good, and thence his falsity he believes to be truth: but every one who

is in good and thence in truth from confirmation and life, can know what evil and falsity are. The reason is this: every good and its truth are in their essence heavenly; and if any is not heavenly in its essence, it is still from a heavenly origin: but every evil and its falsity are in their essence infernal; and what is not infernal in its essence, is still thence by origin: and everything heavenly is in light; but everything infernal, in darkness. H. D. 11–19.

[See A. C. 668, 671, 678–680, 1577, 1614, 1904, 1941, 1950, 1997, 2173, 2184, 2190, 2425, 2429, 2434, 2508, 2531, 2572, 2588, 2623, 2781, 2831, 2904, 3033, 3049, 3101, 3110, 3116, 3179, 3300, 3308, 3316, 3324, 3325, 3387, 3402, 3513, 3540, 3570, 3584, 3607, 3610, 3623, 3659, 3691, 3703, 3704, 3726, 3793, 3865, 3952, 3986, 4005, 4067, 4154, 4205, 4301, 4380, 4390, 4581, 4796, 4906, 5232, 5704, 5912, 6065, 7564, 7887, 8349, 9079, 9637, 9667, 9832, 10,122, 10,334, 10,618; A. E. 136, 152, 292, 386, 478, 536, 638, 725, 741; T. C. R. 38, 87, 105, 142, 145, 245, 249, 250, 367, 397, 398, 624, 660.]

CHAPTER VI.

CONCERNING THE WILL AND THE UNDERSTANDING.

If any one will DO His WILL, he shall KNOW of the DOCTRINE, whether it be of GOD, or whether I speak of myself. John vii. 17.

If ye KNOW these things, happy are ye if ye DO them. John xiii. 17.

FROM THE NEW JERUSALEM AND ITS HEAVENLY DOCTRINE, BY EMANUEL SWEDENBORG.

MAN has two faculties which make his life: the one is called the WILL, and the other the UNDERSTANDING. They are distinct from each other, but so created that they are one; and when one, they are called the MIND. Wherefore they are the human mind; and all man's life is therein.

2. As all things in the universe which are according to Divine Order refer themselves to Good and Truth, so do all things in man to the Will and the Understanding; since good in man is of his will, and truth in him is of his understanding. For these two faculties, or these two lives of man, are the receptacles and sub-

jects of the former: the will is the receptacle and the subject of all things of good, and the understanding is the receptacle and the subject of all things of truth: Goods and truths with man are nowhere else. And because the goods and truths in man are nowhere else, thus neither are love and faith anywhere else: since love is of good, and good is of love; and faith is of truth, and truth is of faith.

3. Now as all things in the universe refer themselves to good and truth, and all things of the church to the good of love and the truth of faith; and as man is man from those two faculties; therefore they also are treated of in this Doctrine: otherwise no distinct idea could be had by man concerning them, nor could thought have a foundation.

4. The will and the understanding also make the spirit of man; for his wisdom and intelligence reside in them, and in general his life. The body is only obedience.

5. Nothing is of more concern to know, than how the will and the understanding make one mind. They make one mind as good and truth make one: for there is a like Marriage between the will and the understanding, as there is between good and truth. What the quality of that marriage is may be fully evident from the things that were set forth above concerning good and truth; namely, that as good is the *esse* itself of a thing, and truth is the *existere* of the thing therefrom; so the will with man is the *esse* itself of his life, and the

understanding the *existere* of life therefrom: for good, which is of the will, forms itself in the understanding, and presents itself to be seen.

6. THEY who are in good and truth have will and understanding: but they who are in evil and falsity have not will and understanding; but for will they have lust, and for understanding they have science: for will truly human is the receptable of good; and understanding the receptacle of truth: wherefore will cannot be said of evil, nor understanding of falsity; because they are opposites: and an opposite destroys. Hence it is, that a man who is in evil and thence in falsity cannot be said to be rational, wise, and intelligent. With the evil, also, the interiors which are of the rational mind, where will and understanding principally reside, are closed. It is believed that the evil also have will and understanding, because they say that they will and that they understand: but their willing is only lusting, and their understanding is only knowing. H. D. 28–33.

[See A. C. 585, 633, 634, 641, 1023, 1043, 1044, 3539, 3619, 3623, 5835, 6608, 7179, 7180, 7503, 8885, 9009, 9069, 9071, 9144, 9175, 9282, 9300, 9942, 9995, 10,064, 10,076, 10,122, 10,109, 10,332; A. E. 295, 466, 666, 785; A. R. 335, 337, 386, 427, 429, 908, 914, 940, 956; T. C. R. 37, 224, 249, 263, 313, 347, 367, 377, 397, 507, 587, 588, 660.]

CHAPTER VII.

CONCERNING THE INTERNAL AND EXTERNAL MAN.

Ye make clean the OUTSIDE of the cup and the platter, but WITHIN they are full of extortion and excess. Cleanse first the INSIDE of the cup and the platter, that the OUTSIDE of them may be clean also. Matt. xxiii. 25, 26.

That which is born of the FLESH is FLESH; and that which is born of the SPIRIT is SPIRIT. John iii. 6.

FROM THE NEW JERUSALEM AND ITS HEAVENLY DOCTRINE, BY EMANUEL SWEDENBORG.

MAN is so created, that he is at the same time in the spiritual world and in the natural world. The spiritual world is where angels are, and the natural world where men are. And since man is so created, there is therefore given to him an Internal and an External, — an internal by which he may be in the spiritual world, and an external by which he may be in the natural world. His internal is what is called the internal man, and his external what is called the external man.

2. Every man has an Internal and an External, but differently with the good and with the evil. With the good the internal is in heaven and its light, and the external in the world and its light; and this light with them is illuminated by the light of heaven: and thus the internal and the external with them act as one, like the efficient cause and the effect, or like the prior and the posterior. But with the evil the internal is in the world and in its light; and the external also is in the same: on which account they see nothing from the light of heaven, but only from the light of the world; which light is called by them the lume [light] of nature. Hence it is that to them the things that are of heaven are in thick-darkness, and those of the world are in light. It is manifest from these things, that the good have an Internal Man and an External Man; but that the evil have not an Internal Man, but only the External.

3. The Internal Man is what is called the Spiritual Man, because it is in the light of heaven, which light is spiritual; and the External Man is what is called the Natural Man, because it is in the light of the world, which light is natural. The man whose internal is in the light of heaven, and his external in the light of the world, is a spiritual man as to both: but the man whose internal is not in the light of heaven, but only in the light of the world, in which his external is also, is a natural man as to both. It is the spiritual man who in the Word is called living, but the natural man who is called dead.

4. THE man whose internal is in the light of heaven, and his external in the light of the world, thinks both spiritually and naturally; but then his spiritual thought flows in into the natural, and is perceived there: but the man whose internal with his external is in the light of the world, does not think spiritually but materially; for he thinks from such things as are in the nature of the world, which are all material. To think spiritually is to think things that are real in themselves, to see truths from the light of truth, and to perceive goods from the love of good; also, to see the qualities of things real, and to perceive their affections, abstractly from matter. But to think materially is to think, to see, and to perceive things together with matter and in matter, thus grossly and obscurely in comparison.

5. THE spiritual internal man, viewed in himself, is an angel of heaven; and while he lives in the body he is also in society with angels, although he does not then know it: and after release from the body, he comes among the angels. But the merely natural internal man, viewed in himself, is a spirit, and not an angel; and is also, while he lives in the body, in society with spirits; but with those that are in hell: he also comes among them, after separation from the body.

6. THE interiors with those who are spiritual men are also actually elevated towards heaven; for they regard that primarily. But with those who are merely

natural, the interiors, which are of the rational mind, are actually turned to the world; because they primarily regard that. With every one, the interiors, which are of the rational mind, are turned to that which he loves above all things; and the exteriors, which are of the natural mind, are turned whither the interiors are.

7. THEY who have only a general idea of the internal and external man, believe that it is the internal man which thinks and which wills, and the external which speaks and which acts; since to think and to will is internal, and to speak and act therefrom is external. But it is to be known, that when a man thinks understandingly and wills wisely, he then thinks and wills from a spiritual internal; but when a man does not think understandingly and will wisely, he thinks and wills from a natural internal: consequently, when a man thinks well concerning the LORD and the things that are of the LORD, and well concerning the neighbor and the things that are of the neighbor, and wills well to them, he then thinks and wills from a spiritual internal; because he then thinks from the faith of truth and from the love of good, thus from heaven. But when a man thinks ill concerning them, and wills ill to them, then he thinks and wills from a natural internal; because from the faith of falsity and from the love of evil, thus from hell. In a word, as far as a man is in love to the LORD and in love towards the neighbor, so far he is in a spiritual internal, and thinks and wills from it,

and from it also speaks and acts: but as far as a man is in the love of self and in the love of the world, so far he is in a natural internal, and thinks and wills from it, and also speaks and acts from it.

8. It is thus provided and arranged by the Lord, that as far as a man thinks and wills from heaven, so far the spiritual internal man is opening and forming: the opening is into heaven even to the Lord, and the formation is according to the things which are of heaven. But, on the other hand, so far as a man does not think and will from heaven but from the world, so far the spiritual internal man is closing, and the external is opening: the opening is into the world, and the formation is to those things that are of the world.

9. Those with whom the spiritual internal man is opened into heaven to the Lord, are in the light of heaven, and in illumination from the Lord, and thence in intelligence and wisdom therefrom: these see truth because it is truth, and perceive good because it is good. But they with whom the spiritual internal man is closed, do not know that there is an internal man, still less what the internal man is; neither do they believe that there is a Divine, nor that there is a life after death, thus neither the things which are of heaven and the church: and because they are only in the light of the world, and in illumination therefrom, they believe in nature as the Divine, see falsity as truth, and perceive evil as good.

10. A MAN is called sensual, whose internal is so far external, that he believes nothing but what he can see with the eyes and touch with the hands. He is the lowest natural man, and is in fallacies concerning all the things which are of the faith of the church.

11. THE internal and external which are treated of, are the internal and external of the spirit of man. His body is only an external superadded, within which they exist: for the body acts nothing from itself, but from its spirit which is in it. It is to be known, that the spirit of man, after release from the body, equally thinks and wills, and speaks and does. To think and will is its internal, and to speak and do is its external: as may be seen in the work on "Heaven and Hell," n. 234–245, 265–275, 432–444, 453–484. H. D. 36–46.

[See A. C. 978, 1563, 1568, 1577, 1587, 1590, 1594, 1598, 1999, 3167, 5786, 5883, 6275, 6322, 8742–8747, 9380, 9701–9709, 10,134, 10,156, 10,396, 10,489, 10,492, 10,602, 10,683; A. E. 475, 654; T. C. R. 109, 154, 188, 326, 340, 374, 399, 401, 410, 420, 443, 454, 596.]

CHAPTER VIII.

CONCERNING LOVE IN GENERAL.

Where your treasure is, there will your HEART be also. Matt. vi. 21.

Out of the abundance of the HEART the mouth speaketh. Matt. xii. 34.

FROM THE NEW JERUSALEM AND ITS HEAVENLY DOCTRINE, BY EMANUEL SWEDENBORG.

THE very life of man is his love: and such as the love is, such is the life; yea, such is the whole man. But it is the ruling or reigning love, that makes the man. This love has many loves subordinate to it, which are derivations. These appear under another guise; but still they are each in the ruling love, and make one kingdom with it. The ruling love is as their king and head: it directs them; and through them, as through mediate ends, it regards and intends its own end, which is the primary and the last of all; and this as well directly as indirectly. That which is of the ruling love is what is loved above all things.

2. WHAT a man loves above all things is continually

present in his thoughts, and also in his will, and makes his veriest life. As for example: He who loves wealth above all things, whether it be money or possessions, is continually turning in his mind how he may procure it to himself, rejoices inmostly when he acquires it, inmostly grieves when he loses it: his heart is in it. He who loves himself above all things, recalls himself in everything; thinks of himself; speaks of himself; acts for the sake of himself: for his life is a life of self.

3. A MAN has for an end that which he loves above all things: he regards it in each and every thing. It is in his will like the latent flow of a river, which sweeps along and carries away, even when he is doing something else; for it is what animates. Such is the thing which one man explores in another, and also sees; and according to it he either leads him, or acts with him.

4. A MAN is altogether such as the ruling principle of his life is: by this he is distinguished from others; according to this he becomes his heaven, if he is good; and he becomes his hell, if he is evil. It is his very will, his proprium, and his nature; for it is the very *esse* of his life. This, after death, cannot be changed; because it is the man himself.

5. ALL that is delightful, satisfying, and happy comes to every one from his ruling love, and according to it. For a man calls that which he loves delightful, because he feels it: but that which he thinks, and does not love, he may also call delightful; but it is not the delight of his life. What to a man is good, is the de-

light of his love; and what to him is evil, is undelightful.

6. THERE are two loves, from which all goods and truths, as from their very fountains, exist; and there are two loves, from which all evils and falsities are. The two loves from which are all goods and truths, are love to the LORD and love towards the neighbor; and the two loves from which are all evils and falsities, are the love of self and the love of the world. The latter two loves are altogether opposite to the former two loves.

7. THE two loves from which all goods and truths are, which are, as was said, love to the LORD and love towards the neighbor, make heaven with man; wherefore also they reign in heaven: and because they make heaven with man, they also make the church with him. The two loves from which all evils and falsities are, which are, as was said, the love of self and the love of the world, make hell with man; wherefore also they reign in hell.

8. THE two loves from which are all goods and truths, which as was said, are the loves of heaven, do open and form the spiritual internal man, because they reside therein: but the two loves from which all evils and falsities are, do, when they rule, close and destroy the spiritual internal man, and cause man to be natural and sensual, according to the quantity and quality of their dominion. H. D. 54–61.

[For References, see page 216.]

CHAPTER IX.

CONCERNING THE LOVES OF SELF AND THE WORLD.

The evil man out of the EVIL TREASURE OF HIS HEART bringeth forth evil. Luke vi. 45.

They LOVED THE PRAISE OF MEN more than the praise of GOD. John xii. 43.

FROM THE NEW JERUSALEM AND ITS HEAVENLY DOCTRINE, BY EMANUEL SWEDENBORG.

THE Love of Self is, to will well to one's self alone, and not to others except for the sake of one's self; not even to the church, to one's country, to any human society, or to a fellow-citizen; as also to do well to them only for the sake of one's reputation, honor, and glory. Unless it sees these things in the goods which it does to them, it says in its heart, What does it concern? why do this? and what gain is it to me? — and so passes it by. Whence it is manifest, that he who is in the love of self does not love the church, nor his country, nor society, nor a fellow-citizen, nor any good, — but himself alone.

2. A MAN is in the love of self, when, in the things which he thinks and does, he does not consider his neighbor, nor thus the public, still less the LORD, but only himself and his; consequently, when he does all things for the sake of himself and his: and if for the sake of the public and the neighbor, it is only that it may appear.

3. IT is said, *for the sake of himself and his;* for he who loves himself also loves his, — who in particular are his children and grandchildren, and in general all who make one with him, — whom he calls his. To love the latter and the former is also to love himself; for he regards them as if in himself, and himself in them. Among those whom he calls his are also all who praise, honor, and pay court to him.

4. THAT man is in the love of self, who despises his neighbor in comparison with himself; who holds him as an enemy if he does not favor him, and if he does not venerate and look up to him: still more in the love of self is he who on that account holds in hatred and persecutes his neighbor; and more still, he who on that account burns with revenge against him, and desires his destruction. Such at length love to be cruel.

5. IT may be evident what the love of self is, from comparison with heavenly love. Heavenly love is, to love uses for the sake of uses, or goods for the sake of goods; which a man performs to the church, to his country, to human society, and to a fellow-citizen. But he who loves them for the sake of himself, loves them

no otherwise than he does domestics, because they serve him. It follows hence, that he who is in the love of self wishes that the church, his country, human societies, and his fellow-citizens, should serve him, and not he them. He puts himself above them, and them below himself.

6. MOREOVER, as far as one is in heavenly love, which is to love uses and goods, and to be affected with delight of heart when he performs them, so far he is led by the LORD; because that is the love in which He is, and which is from Him. But as far as any one is in the love of self, so far he is led by himself; and as far as he is led by himself, he is led by his proprium: and the proprium of man is nothing but evil; for it is his hereditary evil, which is to love one's self above GOD, and the world above heaven.

7. SUCH also is the love of self, that as far as the reins are loosened to it, that is, so far as external bonds are removed, which are fears of the law and its penalties, and of the loss of reputation, honor, gain, office, and life; so far it rushes on, even till it wishes to have empire not only over the universal world, but also over heaven, and over the Divine Itself. Nowhere is there any bound or end to it. This lurks in every one who is in the love of self, although it is not manifest before the world, where the aforesaid reins and bonds restrain him; and every such one, where he meets with an impossibility, stands fast there, until it becomes possible. All these things show that the man who is in such love

does not know that such insane, unbounded lust lurks within him. Yet that it is so, no one can but see, in potentates and kings, that have not such reins, bonds, and impossibilities; who rush on and subjugate provinces and kingdoms as far as they have success, and aspire to power and glory beyond limits: and still more in those who extend their domination into heaven, and transfer to themselves all the divine power of the LORD, and continually lust for more.

8. THERE are two kinds of rule: the one is that of love towards the neighbor, and the other is that of the love of self. These two kinds of rule are in their essence altogether opposite to each other. He who rules from love towards the neighbor wishes good to all, and loves nothing more than to perform uses, thus to serve others:—to serve others is, from willing well, to do good and perform uses to others. This is his love, and this the delight of his heart. As far, too, as he is elevated to dignities, so far he is also glad; but not for the sake of the dignities, but for the sake of the uses which he can then perform in more abundance and a greater degree. Such is rule in the heavens. But he who rules from the love of self wills good to no one, but only to himself and to his. The uses which he performs are only for the sake of the honor and glory of himself, which to him are the only uses. To him serving others is for the sake of the end that he may be served, honored, and have dominion. He solicits dignities, not for the sake of the goods which he may per-

form, but that he may be in eminence and glory, and thence in the delight of his heart.

9. The love of rule also remains to every one after the life in the world; but to them who have ruled from love towards the neighbor is also intrusted dominion in the heavens: yet it is not they, but the uses and goods, which they love, that then rule; and when uses and goods rule, the Lord rules. But they who in the world have ruled from the love of self, are, after the life in the world, in hell; and are vile slaves there.

10. From these things it is now comprehended, who are in the love of self. But it is of no concern how they appear in the external form, whether elate or submissive: for such things are in the interior man; and the interior man is hidden by most, and the exterior is trained to counterfeit the things which are of love to the public and the neighbor, thus contrary things: and this also for the sake of self. For they know that to love the public and the neighbor affects all interiorly; and that so far themselves are loved and in estimation. Why it affects all, is because heaven flows in into that love.

11. The evils which those have who are in the love of self are in general contempt of others, envy, enmity against those who do not favor them, hostility therefrom, hatreds of various kinds, revenge, cunning, deceit, unmercifulness, and cruelty: and where such evils are, there is also contempt of the Divine, and of divine things, which are the truths and goods of the church;

which if they honor, it is only with the mouth, and not with the heart. And because such evils are thence, similar falsities also are; for falsities are from evils.

12. BUT the Love of the World is, to will to divert to one's self the wealth of others by whatever art, and to place the heart in riches, and to suffer the world to withdraw and lead one away from spiritual love, which is love towards the neighbor; thus away from heaven. In the love of the world are they who desire to divert the goods of others to themselves by various arts,— especially they who do it by cunning and deceits, making nothing of the good of the neighbor. They who are in that love covet the goods of others; and as far as they do not fear the laws and the loss of reputation on account of lucre, they deprive, yea, rob them.

13. BUT the Love of the World is not opposite to heavenly love to such a degree as the love of self is, since so great evils are not concealed in it. That love is manifold: there is the love of wealth, that one may be elevated to honors: there is the love of honors and dignities, that one may gain wealth: there is the love of wealth for the sake of the various uses from which one enjoys delights in the world: there is the love of wealth for the sake of wealth alone, — such love have the avaricious, — and so on. The end for the sake of which wealth is loved, is called use; and the end or use is that from which a love derives its quality: for the love is such as the end is for the sake of which it is cherished: other things serve it as means.

14. In a word, the love of self and the love of the world are altogether opposite to love to the Lord and love towards the neighbor. Wherefore the love of self and the love of the world are infernal loves, reign also in hell, and likewise make hell with man. But love to the Lord and love towards the neighbor are heavenly loves, reign also in heaven, and likewise make heaven with man.

15. From these things which have now been said, it may be seen that in the two former loves, and from them, are all evils; for the evils which were enumerated above (par. 11) are general: the rest, which were not enumerated because they are specific, are derived and flow from those. It may hence be evident, that man, because he is born into those two loves, is born into evils of every kind.

16. For a man to know evils, he ought to know their origins: and unless he knows evils, he cannot know goods, thus cannot know what he is. Hence it is, that those two origins of evils have been here treated of. H. D. 65–80.

[See A. C. 33, 693, 694, 760, 1307, 1308, 1505, 1506, 1594, 1668, 1691, 1862, 2041, 2057, 2122, 2219, 2444, 3610, 4750, 4751, 4776, 5721, 6667, 7178, 7255, 7366–7377, 7488, 7494, 8318, 8487, 8676, 8995, 9210, 10,731, 10,741–10,749; T. C. R. 394–405, 662; A. E. 584, 653, 982, 1022; H. H. 551–565.]

CHAPTER X.

CONCERNING LOVE TOWARDS THE NEIGHBOR, OR CHARITY.

A new Commandment I give unto you, That ye LOVE one another: as I HAVE LOVED YOU, that ye also LOVE ONE ANOTHER. By this shall all know that ye are MY disciples, if ye have LOVE ONE TO ANOTHER. John xiii. 34, 35.

FROM THE NEW JERUSALEM AND ITS HEAVENLY DOCTRINE, BY EMANUEL SWEDENBORG.

IT shall first be told what the NEIGHBOR is; since it is he who is to be loved, and towards whom Charity is to be exercised. For, unless it is known what the neighbor is, charity may be exercised in the same manner, without distinction, towards the evil equally as towards the good; whence charity becomes not charity: for the evil, for goods done, do evil to the neighbor; but the good do good.

2. IT is a common opinion at this day, that every man is equally the Neighbor; and that good is to be done to every one who is in need of help. But it

concerns Christian prudence to scrutinize well what a man's life is, and to exercise charity according to that. The man of the internal church does this with discrimination, thus with understanding; but the man of the external church, because he cannot so discern real things, does it indiscriminately.

3. THE distinctions of the neighbor, which the man of the church ought by all means to know, are determined according to the good that is with every one: and because all good proceeds from the LORD, the LORD is the Neighbor in the supreme sense and in a supereminent degree; from whom is the origin. Hence it follows, that, as much of the LORD as any one has in himself, so far he is the neighbor: and because no one receives the LORD, that is, the good which is from Him, in the same measure as another, for that reason one is not the neighbor in the same measure as another. For all who are in the heavens, and all who are good on the earth, differ in goodness. Nowhere is there given with two a good altogether one and the same: it must be various, that every kind may subsist by itself. But all those varieties, thus all the distinctions of neighbor, which are determined according to the reception of the LORD, that is, according to the reception of good from Him, no man anywhere, not even an angel, can know, — but only in general, — thus the genera and their species. Nor does the LORD require more from the man of the church, than that he should live according to that which he knows.

4. BECAUSE the good in every one is various, it follows thence that the quality of the good determines in what degree and in what proportion any one is the Neighbor. That it is so, is manifest from the Lord's parable concerning him who fell among thieves; whom, though half-dead, the Priest passed by, and also the Levite. But the Samaritan, after he had bound up his wounds, and poured in oil and wine, took him up upon his own beast, and brought him to an inn, and made arrangements that care should be taken of him. This one, because he exercised the good of Charity, is called the Neighbor. Luke x. 29–37. It may hence be known, that they who are in good are the Neighbor. Oil and wine, which the Samaritan poured into the wounds, also signify good and its truth.

5. IT is manifest from the things here said, that in a universal sense, Good is the Neighbor; because a man is the neighbor according to the quality of the good which is with him from the LORD. And because good is the neighbor, so is love; for all good is of love. Thus every man is the neighbor according to the quality of the love which he has from the LORD.

6. THAT it is love that makes one to be the neighbor, and that every one is the neighbor according to the quality of his love, is clearly manifest from those who are in the love of self. They recognize as neighbor those that love them most; that is, as far as they are theirs, they embrace them, kiss them, do good to them, and call them brethren; yea, because they are

evil, they say that these are the neighbor above others. The rest they hold for neighbor as they love them, thus according to the quality and quantity of the love. Such derive the origin of the neighbor from themselves, for the reason that the love makes and determines it. But they who do not love themselves above others, — and such are all who are of the LORD's kingdom, — will derive the origin of the neighbor from Him whom they ought to love above all things, thus from the LORD: and they will hold every one as the neighbor, according to the quality of his love to Him and from Him. From these things it is clear, whence the origin of the neighbor is to be derived by the man of the church; and that every one is the neighbor according to the good which he has from the LORD, thus good itself.

7. THAT it is so, the LORD also teaches in Matthew: for He said to them that were in good, that they "gave Him to eat, that they gave Him to drink, took Him in, clothed Him, visited Him, and came to Him in prison: and then, that as much as they did to one of His least brethren, they did to Him." xxv. 34–40. In these six kinds of good, understood in the spiritual sense, are comprehended all the kinds of neighbor. It is hence manifest also, that when good is loved, the LORD is loved; for the LORD is He from whom good is, who is in good, and who is good itself.

8. BUT not only is man individually the neighbor, but also man collectively: for a Society, greater or less, is so; one's Country is; the Church is; the LORD's

Kingdom is; and above them all, the LORD Himself is. These are the Neighbor to whom one must do good from love. These degrees of the neighbor are also ascending: for a Society of many is so in a higher degree than an individual man; in a still higher degree is one's Country; in a still higher degree the Church is; and in a degree still higher the LORD's Kingdom is; but in the highest the LORD is. These ascending degrees are like the steps of a ladder, at the top of which is the LORD.

9. A SOCIETY is the Neighbor above an individual man, because it consists of many. Towards it charity is to be exercised in like manner as towards an individual man; namely, according to the quality of the good which is in it: thus altogether otherwise towards a society of the upright, than towards a society of the un-upright. A Society is loved, when its good is provided for from the love of good.

10. ONE'S Country is the Neighbor above a Society, because it is like a parent: for there a man was born; it nourishes him, and protects him from injuries. Good is to be done to one's country from love according to its necessities, which principally regard its sustenance, and the civil life and spiritual life of those who are there. He who loves his country, and does good to it from good-will, in the other life loves the LORD's kingdom; for there the LORD's kingdom is his country: and he who loves the LORD's kingdom loves the LORD; because the LORD is the all in all of his kingdom.

11. The Church is the Neighbor above one's Country; for he who provides for the Church, provides for the souls and the eternal life of the men who are in his country. Wherefore, he who provides for the Church from love, loves the neighbor in a higher degree; since he desires and wishes heaven and happiness of life to eternity to others.

12. The Lord's Kingdom is the Neighbor in a still higher degree; for the Lord's kingdom consists of all who are in good, as well those on the earth as those in the heavens: thus the Lord's kingdom is Good with all its quality in the complex. When this is loved, the individuals are loved who are in good.

13. These are the degrees of the Neighbor; and with those who are in love towards the neighbor, the love ascends according to these degrees. But these degrees are degrees in successive order, in which the prior or superior is to be preferred to the posterior or inferior: and because the Lord is in the highest, and as He is to be regarded in each of the degrees as the end to which [they look], so He is to be loved above all persons and all things. It may now be evident from these things, how love to the Lord conjoins itself with love towards the Neighbor.

14. It is a common remark, that every one is neighbor to himself; that is, that every one should first provide for himself: but the Doctrine of Charity teaches how this is to be understood. Every one should provide for himself, that he may have the necessaries of

life; namely, food, clothing, habitation, and other things which are necessarily required in the civil life in which he is; and this not only for himself, but also for his [family]; nor for the present time only, but for the time to come also: since, unless one procures for himself the necessaries of life, he cannot be in a state to exercise charity; for he is in want of all things.

15. BUT how each one ought to be neighbor to himself, may be evident from this comparison: Every one ought to provide food and clothing for his body: this must be the first thing, but to the end that there may be a sound mind in a sound body. And every one ought to provide food for his mind; namely, such things as are of intelligence and wisdom; to the end that it may thereby be in a state to serve his fellow-citizen, human society, his country, and the Church, — thus the LORD. He who does this, provides well for himself to eternity. It is hence manifest that the first thing is [to know] where the end is for the sake of which [one lives]; for to that all things look. This presents itself also like as one who is building a house. He first lays the foundation; but the foundation will be for the house, and the house for residence. He who believes he is neighbor to himself in the foremost place is like him who regards the foundation as the end, not the house and residence: when yet residence is itself the first and last end; and the house, with the foundation, is only the means to the end.

16. THE end evinces how every one must be neigh-

bor to himself, and provide first for himself. If the end is, to become rich above others only for the sake of riches, or for the sake of pleasure, or for the sake of eminence, and for like things, it is an evil end; and he does not love his neighbor, but himself. But if the end is, to procure wealth to himself, that he may be in a state to provide for his fellow-citizen, for human society, for his country, and for the Church, in like manner as he procures for himself offices for the same end, he loves the neighbor. The end itself for the sake of which he acts, makes the man; since the end is his love: for every one has for his first and last end what he loves above all things.

These things have been said concerning the Neighbor: love towards him, or CHARITY, shall now be spoken of.

17. IT is believed by many, that love towards the neighbor is, to give to the poor, to afford help to the needy, and to do good to every one. But Charity is, to act prudently, and for the sake of the end that good may come. He who affords help to any poor or needy evil-doer, through him does evil to the neighbor: for, by the help which he affords, he confirms him in evil, and supplies him with the means of doing evil to others. Not so he who affords assistance to the good.

18. BUT Charity extends itself much more widely than to the poor and needy; for Charity is, to do right in every work, and duty in every service. If a Judge does justice for the sake of justice, he exercises charity:

if he punishes the guilty, and clears the innocent, he exercises charity: for he thus seeks good to his fellow-citizen, and seeks good to his country. A Priest, who teaches truth and leads to good for the sake of truth and good, exercises charity. But he who does such things for the sake of himself and the world, does not exercise charity; because he does not love his neighbor, but himself.

19. It is the same with the rest, whether they are in any office, or are not: as with children towards their parents, and with parents towards their children; with servants towards their masters, and with masters towards servants; with subjects towards the king, and with the king towards his subjects. He of them who does duty from duty, and justice from justice, exercises charity.

20. Why these things are of love towards the Neighbor, or Charity, is because, as was said above, every man is the neighbor, but in different ways. A Society, less or greater, is more the neighbor; one's Country still more the neighbor; the Lord's Kingdom still more; and the Lord above them all: and, in a universal sense, good, which proceeds from the Lord, is the neighbor; consequently also sincerity and justice is. On which account, he who does any good whatever for the sake of good, and who acts sincerely and justly for the sake of sincerity and justice, loves the neighbor, and exercises charity: for he does it from the love of goodness, sincerity, and justice, and thence from the

love of those in whom goodness, sincerity, and justice are.

21. Charity, therefore, is the internal affection from which a man wills to do good, and this without remuneration. It is the delight of his life to do it. With those who do good from an internal affection, charity is in everything which they think and speak, and which they will and do. It may be said that a man, and an angel, as to his interiors, is Charity, when to him good is the neighbor. So widely does Charity extend itself.

22. They to whom the loves of self and the world are for an end, can by no means be in charity. They do not even know what charity is; and do not at all comprehend, that to will and do good to the neighbor, without the end of reward, is heaven in man; and that in that affection is a happiness as great as is that of the angels of heaven, which is ineffable. For they believe that if they are deprived of the joy [that comes] from the glory of honors and wealth, nothing of joy is any longer to be had: when yet heavenly joy then first begins; which infinitely transcends. H. D. 84–105.

[See T. C. R. 392–462; A. C. 615, 3773, 3887, 3938, 4741, 4766, 5859, 6627–6633, 6703–6712, 6818–6824, 6933–6938, 7038, 7080–7086, 7178–7182, 7197, 7255–7263, 7366–7377, 7623–7627, 7752–7762, 7814–7821, 8033–8037, 8120–8124, 8252–8257; A. E. 104, 212, 324, 444, 644, 918, 932–934; D. C. 1–125; L. 1–114.]

CHAPTER XI.

CONCERNING FAITH.

God so loved the world, that He gave His only-begotten Son, that every one that BELIEVETH in Him should not perish, but have everlasting life. He that BELIEVETH on Him is not judged: but he that BELIEVETH NOT is judged already, because he HATH NOT BELIEVED in the name of the only-begotten Son of God. And this is the judgment, that the light has come into the world, and men loved the darkness rather than the light, because their WORKS WERE EVIL. For every one that PRACTISETH EVIL THINGS HATETH THE LIGHT, and cometh not to the light, lest HIS WORKS should be reproved. But he that DOETH THE TRUTH cometh to the light, that HIS WORKS may be made manifest, that they are WROUGHT IN GOD. John iii. 16–21.

FROM THE NEW JERUSALEM AND ITS HEAVENLY DOCTRINE, BY EMANUEL SWEDENBORG.

NO one can know what Faith is in its essence, unless he knows what Charity is; since where there is not charity, there there is not faith: for charity makes one with faith, as good does with truth. For, what a man loves, or what he holds dear, this to him is good; and what a man believes, this to him is truth. It is hence manifest, that there is a like union of charity and faith, as there is of good and truth. What the quality of the union is, may be evident from the things which were said above concerning GOOD and TRUTH.

2. SUCH also is the union of Charity and Faith as is that of the Will and the Understanding with man: for it is these two faculties which receive good and truth; the will, good; and the understanding, truth. So also do these two faculties receive charity and faith; since good is of charity, and truth is of faith. That charity and faith are with man and in him, no one is ignorant; and since they are with him and in him, they are nowhere but in his will and understanding: for all the life of man is therein, and is thence. Man also has memory: but this is only the ante-room, where those things are collected which are to enter into the will and the understanding. Hence it is manifest, that there is a like union of charity and faith, as there is of the will and the understanding. What this union is may be evident from the things that were said before of the WILL and the UNDERSTANDING.

3. CHARITY conjoins itself with faith in man, when the man wills that which he knows and perceives: to will is of charity, and to know and perceive are of faith. Faith enters into a man, and becomes his, when he wills and loves that which he knows and perceives: previously it is out of him.

4. FAITH does not become faith with man, unless it becomes spiritual; and it does not become spiritual, unless it becomes of the love: and it then becomes of the love, when man loves to live truth and good; that is, to live according to the things which are commanded in the WORD.

5. FAITH is the affection of truth from willing truth because it is truth; and to will truth because it is truth, is the spiritual itself of man: for it is abstracted from the natural, which is to will truth not for the sake of truth, but for the sake of one's glory, reputation, or gain. Truth abstracted from such things is spiritual, because it is from the Divine. What proceeds from the Divine is spiritual; and this is conjoined to man by love: for love is spiritual conjunction.

6. A MAN may know, think, and understand much; but the things which do not agree with his love he rejects from himself, when, being left to himself alone, he is meditating: and therefore also he rejects them after the life of the body, when he is in the spirit. For that alone remains in a man's spirit, which has entered into his love: the other things are, after death, regarded as foreign; which, because they are not of his love, he casts out of the house. It is said, *in a man's spirit*, because man lives a spirit after death.

7. AN idea of the good which is of charity, and of the truth which is of faith, may be formed from the light and heat of the sun. When the light which proceeds from the sun is conjoined with heat, which occurs

in the time of spring and summer, then all things of the Earth germinate and bloom: but when there is not heat in the light, as in the time of winter, then all things of the Earth are torpid and die. Spiritual light also is the truth of faith, and spiritual heat is love. From these things an idea can be formed concerning the man of the church, — of what quality he is, when faith with him is conjoined to charity, — namely, that he is like a garden and a paradise; and of what quality he is, when with him faith is not conjoined to charity,— that he is like a desert, and a land covered with snow.

8. THE confidence or trust which is said to be of faith, and is called saving faith itself, is not a spiritual confidence or trust, but a natural one, when it is of faith alone. Spiritual confidence or trust has its essence and life from the good of love, but not from the truth of faith separate: the confidence of faith separate is dead. On which account true confidence cannot be given with those who lead an evil life. The confidence also that salvation is on account of the LORD's merit with the FATHER, whatever a man's life had been, is not from the truth. All who are in spiritual faith have confidence that they are saved by the LORD: for they believe that the LORD came into the world to give eternal life to those who believe and live according to the commandments which He taught; and that He regenerates these, and renders them fit for heaven; and that He alone does this, without man's help, from pure mercy.

9. To believe the things which the WORD teaches,

or which the Doctrine of the Church teaches, and not to live according to them, appears as if it were faith; and some also imagine that they will be saved by it. But by that alone no one is saved: for it is Persuasive Faith; and what its quality is shall now be told.

10. FAITH is persuasive, when the WORD and the Doctrine of the Church are believed and loved, not for the sake of the truth, and a life according to it, but for the sake of gain, honor, and the reputation of learning, as ends. On which account they who are in that faith do not look to the LORD and to heaven, but to themselves and to the world. They who in the world aspire to great things and desire many, are in a stronger persuasion that what the doctrine of the church teaches is the truth, than they who do not aspire to great and desire many things. The cause is, that to them the doctrine of the church is only a means to their ends; and as far as the ends are desired, so far the means are loved, and are also believed. But the reality in itself is this: as far as they are in the fire of the loves of self and the world, and speak, preach, and act from that fire, so far they are in that persuasion; and they then know no otherwise, than that it is so. But when they are not in the fire of those loves, they then believe little; and many not at all. It is hence manifest, that persuasive faith is a faith of the mouth, and not of the heart; thus that in itself it is not faith.

11. THEY who are in persuasive faith do not know from any internal illustration, whether the things which

they teach are true or false; yea, neither do they care, provided they are believed by the people: for they are in no affection for truth for the sake of truth. On which account, if they are deprived of honors and gains, they recede from faith, provided reputation be not perilled. For persuasive faith is not interiorly with man, but stands without, only in the memory; from which it is brought forth when it is taught. Wherefore also that faith, with its truths, vanishes after death: for then there remains of faith only that which is interiorly in man; that is, which is enrooted in good; thus which has become of the life.

12. THEY who are in persuasive faith, are understood by these in Matthew: "Many will say to ME in that day, LORD, LORD, have we not prophesied by Thy name, and by Thy name cast out demons, and in Thy name done many virtues? But then I will confess to them, I know you not, ye workers of iniquity." vii. 22, 23. Also in Luke: "Then shall ye begin to say, We have eaten and drunk before Thee; and Thou hast taught in our streets: but He will say, I say unto you, I know you not whence ye are: depart from ME, all ye workers of iniquity." xiii. 26, 27. They are also understood by the five foolish virgins, who had not oil in their lamps, in Matthew: "Afterwards came those virgins, saying, LORD, LORD, open to us: but He answering shall say, Verily I say unto you, I know you not." xxv. 11, 12. Oil in the lamps is the good of love in faith. H. D. 108–119. [For Ref. see p. 216.]

CHAPTER XII.

CONCERNING PIETY.

Men ought always to pray. Luke xviii. 1.

Not every one that SAITH unto ME, LORD, LORD, shall enter into the kingdom of the heavens; but HE THAT DOETH THE WILL of My FATHER who is in the heavens. Matt. vii. 21.

FROM THE NEW JERUSALEM AND ITS HEAVENLY DOCTRINE, BY EMANUEL SWEDENBORG.

IT is believed by many, that spiritual life, or the life that leads to heaven, consists in *Piety*, in *external Sanctity*, and in the *Renunciation of the world.* But piety without charity, and external sanctity without internal, and the renunciation of the world without a life in the world, do not make spiritual life: but piety from charity, external sanctity from internal sanctity, and the renunciation of the world with a life in the world, do make it.

2. PIETY is, to think and speak piously; to devote much time to prayers; to behave one's self humbly then; to frequent temples, and to listen devoutly to the

preachings there; and often yearly to attend the Sacrament of the Supper, and in like manner the other services of worship according to the statutes of the Church. But a life of charity is, to will well and do well to the neighbor; in every work to act from justice and equity, from good and truth; and the same in every function: in a word, a life of charity consists in performing uses. In the latter life Divine Worship primarily consists; but in the former, secondarily. For which cause, he who separates the one from the other, — namely, he who lives a life of piety, and not at the same time a life of charity, — does not worship GOD. He thinks indeed of GOD; yet not from GOD, but from himself: for he continually thinks of himself, and nought of his neighbor, — and if of his neighbor, he holds him in low esteem if he is not also such and such. And he thinks also of heaven as a reward: thence in his mind is merit, and also the love of self, as also contempt or neglect of uses, and thus of the neighbor; and at the same time there is a belief of his blamelessness. It may hence be evident, that a life of piety separated from a life of charity is not the spiritual life which must be in divine worship. Compare Matt. vi. 7, 8.

3. LIKE to such piety is external Sanctity. But this is not holy in a man, unless his internal is holy; for such as a man is as to his internal, such is he as to the external: for the latter proceeds from the former, as action does from its spirit. Wherefore external sanctity without internal sanctity is natural and not spir-

itual. Hence it is, that it is had equally with the evil as with the good: and they who place all worship in it, are for the most part empty; that is, without the knowledges of good and truth: and yet goods and truths are the very sanctities which are to be known, believed, and loved, because they are from the Divine; and thus the Divine is in them. Internal sanctity is, therefore, to love good and truth for the sake of good and truth, and justice and sincerity for the sake of justice and sincerity. As far as a man thus loves these, so far he is spiritual; and his worship also is so: for so far he also wills to know them and to do them. But as far as a man does not thus love them, so far he is natural, and his worship also; and so far also he does not will to know them and to do them. External worship without internal may be compared with the life of the respiration without the life of the heart; but external worship from internal, with the life of the respiration conjoined to the life of the heart.

4. But as regards the Renunciation of the world, it is believed by many, that to renounce the world, and to live in the spirit and not in the flesh, is to reject worldly things, which are chiefly riches and honors; and to go on continually in pious meditation about God, about salvation, and about eternal life; and to pass life in prayers, in the reading of the Word, and of pious books; and also to afflict one's self. But these things are not renouncing the world; but to renounce the world is to love God and to love the neigh-

bor: and God is loved, when one lives according to his commandments; and the neighbor is loved, when a man performs uses. Wherefore, that a man may receive the life of heaven, he must by all means live in the world, and in services and business there. A life withdrawn from worldly things is a life of thought and faith separated from a life of love and charity; in which life willing good and doing good to the neighbor perishes: and when this perishes, spiritual life is like a house without a foundation; which gradually either sinks down, or opens and spreads into chinks, or totters even till it falls to pieces.

5. That to do good is to worship the Lord, is evident from the Lord's words: "Every one that heareth My words, and doeth them, I will liken to a prudent man, who built a house upon a rock: but him that heareth My words, and doeth them not, I will liken to a foolish man, who built a house upon the sand, or upon the ground without a foundation." Matt. vii. 24–27; Luke vi. 47–49.

6. It is now manifest from these things, that a life of Piety so far has value, and is acceptable to the Lord, as a life of charity is conjoined to it: for this is the primary; and such as this is, such is that. Also, that external Sanctity so far has value, and is acceptable to the Lord, as it proceeds from internal sanctity; for, as is the latter, such is the former. As also, that the Renunciation of the world so far has value, and is acceptable to the Lord, as this is done in the

world: for they renounce the world, who remove the love of self and the world, and act justly and sincerely in every function, in every business, and in every work, from an interior, thus from a heavenly origin; which origin is in that life, when a man acts well, sincerely, and justly, because this is according to the divine laws. H. D. 123–128.

[See A. C. 1102, 1151, 1153, 5066, 5067, 8252–8257; D. C. 1–125; L. 1–114; C. L. 3, 9.]

CHAPTER XIII.

CONCERNING CONSCIENCE.

All things whatsoever YE WOULD that men should do to you, SO ALSO DO YE to them: for this is the Law and the Prophets. Matt. vii. 12.

And why even of yourselves JUDGE YE NOT what is JUST? Luke xii. 57.

FROM THE NEW JERUSALEM AND ITS HEAVENLY DOCTRINE, BY EMANUEL SWEDENBORG.

CONSCIENCE is formed with a man from the religion in which he is, according to the reception of it interiorly in himself.

2. CONSCIENCE, with the man of the Church, is formed by the truths of faith from the WORD, or from Doctrine out of the WORD, according to the reception of them in the heart: for, when a man knows the truths of faith, and comprehends them in his measure, and then wills them and does them, conscience is then formed in him. Reception in the heart is in the will; for it is the will of man which is called the heart. Hence it is, that they who have conscience speak from

the heart the things they speak, and do from the heart the things they do. They also have the mind not divided: for, according to that which they understand and believe to be true and good, they do.

3. WITH those who are enlightened in the truths of faith above others, and who are in clear perception above others, a more perfect conscience can be given, than with those who are less enlightened, and are in obscure perception.

4. IN a true conscience is the life itself of the spiritual man; for therein is his faith conjoined to charity: on which account, to such, to do from conscience is to do from their spiritual life, and to do contrary to conscience is to do contrary to that spiritual life of theirs. It is hence that they are in the tranquillity of peace, and in internal blessedness, when they do according to conscience; and in intranquillity and pain, when they do contrary to it. It is this pain, which is called remorse of conscience.

5. MAN has a conscience of what is good and a conscience of what is just. The conscience of good is the conscience of the internal man, and the conscience of justice is the conscience of the external man. The conscience of what is good is to do according to the precepts of faith from an internal affection, but the conscience of what is just is to do according to the civil and moral laws from an external affection. They who have the conscience of good have also the conscience of justice; but they who have only the conscience of

what is just, are in the ability to receive the conscience of what is good, and also do receive it when instructed.

6. CONSCIENCE, with those who are in charity towards the neighbor, is the conscience of truth, because it is formed by the faith of truth; but with those who are in love to the LORD, it is the conscience of good, because it is formed by the love of truth. The conscience of the latter is a higher conscience, and is called the perception of truth from good. They who have the conscience of truth are of the LORD's spiritual kingdom; but they who have the higher conscience, which is called perception, are of the LORD's celestial kingdom.

7. BUT let examples illustrate what conscience is. He who has by him another's goods without the other's knowledge, and can thus gain them without fear of the law, or of the loss of honor and reputation, — if he still restores them to the other because they are not his, — he has conscience: for he does good for the sake of good, and justice for the sake of justice. Suppose also one who is able to obtain an office, but knows that another, who also seeks it, would be more useful to his country, — if he gives place to the other for the sake of his country's good, — he has a good conscience: — and so in other cases.

8. IT may from these things be concluded, of what quality those are who have not conscience. They are known from the opposite: as, — they who for the sake of any gain whatever make what is unjust appear to be

just, and evil appear to be good, and the reverse, — they have not conscience. Neither do they know what conscience is: and if they are instructed what it is, they do not believe; and some are not willing to know. Such are they who act in all things for the sake of themselves and the world.

9. THEY who did not receive conscience in the world cannot receive conscience in the other life; thus they cannot be saved. This is because they have not a plane into which heaven may flow, and through which it may operate, — that is, the LORD through heaven, and lead them to himself: for conscience is the plane and receptacle of the influx of heaven. H. D. 130-138.

[See also, A. C. 227, 827, 831, 847, 863, 865, 950, 965, 977, 986, 1023, 1043, 1076, 1077, 1835, 1862, 1914, 1919, 1935, 2053, 2063, 2144, 2380, 2515, 2759, 2842, 2915, 4167, 4299, 4328, 4390, 4459, 4493, 5145, 5386, 5470, 5724, 6207, 6213, 6208, 6367, 7217, 7490, 7935, 8042, 8081, 8521, 9112-9122, 9596, 9935, 9995, 10,124, 10,296; T. C. R. 666.]

CHAPTER XIV.

CONCERNING FREEDOM.

JESUS said, If ye continue in My WORD, ye are My disciples indeed. And ye shall know the TRUTH; and the TRUTH shall make you FREE. If the SON therefore shall make you FREE, ye shall be FREE indeed. John viii. 31, 32, 36.

FROM THE NEW JERUSALEM AND ITS HEAVENLY DOCTRINE, BY EMANUEL SWEDENBORG.

ALL Freedom is of love; for that which a man loves he does freely. Hence also all freedom is of the will; for that which a man loves he also wills: and since love and will make the life of man, freedom also makes it. It may from these things be evident what freedom is; namely, that it is that which is of the love and the will, and thence of the life of man. Hence it is, that that which a man does from freedom appears to him as if it were from his proprium.

2. To do evil from freedom appears as if free, but it is slavery; because that freedom is from the love

of self and the love of the world: and these loves are from hell. Such freedom is also actually turned into slavery after death; for a man who had such freedom then becomes a vile slave in hell. But to do good from freedom is freedom itself, because it is from love to the LORD and love towards the neighbor; and these loves are from heaven. This freedom also remains after death, and then becomes truly freedom: for a man who had such freedom becomes in heaven like a son of the house. This the LORD thus teaches: "Every one that doeth sin is the servant of sin: the servant remaineth not in the house for ever; the son remaineth for ever: if the SON shall make you free, ye will be truly free." John viii. 34–36. Now since all good is from the LORD, and all evil from hell, it follows that it is freedom to be led by the LORD, and slavery to be led by hell.

3. WHY man has the freedom of thinking what is evil and false, and also of doing it, so far as the laws do not restrain, is for the reason that he may be able to be reformed: for goods and truths, that they may become of his life, must be implanted in his love and will; and this cannot be done, unless he has freedom of thinking what is evil and false as well as what is good and true. This freedom is given by the LORD to every man: and, when he is thinking what is good and true, as far as he does not then love evil and falsity, so far the LORD implants the former in his love and will, thus in his life, and so reforms him.

That which is inseminated in freedom also remains; but that which is inseminated in compulsion does not remain: because what is compelled is not from the man's will, but from the will of him who compels. It is also hence, that worship from freedom is pleasing to the LORD; but not worship from compulsion: for worship from freedom is worship from love; but not so worship from compulsion.

4. THE freedom of doing good and the freedom of doing evil, although in external aspect they appear alike, are as different and distant from each other as heaven and hell. The freedom of doing good is also from heaven, and is called heavenly freedom; but the freedom of doing evil is from hell, and is called infernal freedom. As far also as a man is in the one, so far he is not in the other; for no one can serve two masters, Matt. vi. 24: which is also manifest from hence, — that those who are in infernal freedom believe that it is slavery and compulsion not to be permitted to will evil and think what is false at their liking; but that they who are in heavenly freedom have a horror at willing evil and thinking what is false; and if they were compelled to them, would be tortured.

5. SINCE to do from freedom appears to a man as if it were from his proprium, hence heavenly freedom may also be called the heavenly proprium; and infernal freedom may be called the infernal proprium. The infernal proprium is that into which man is born;

and it is evil: but the heavenly proprium is that into which a man is reformed; and it is good.

6. It may be evident from these things, what Free Agency is; namely, that it is to do good from self-decision or from the will; and that they are in that freedom, who are led by the Lord: and they are led by the Lord, who love good and truth for the sake of good and truth.

7. A man may know which kind of freedom he is in, from the delight he feels, while he is thinking, speaking, doing, hearing, and seeing; for all delight is of the love. H. D. 141–147.

[See also, A. C. 892, 905, 1937, 1947, 2744, 2870–2893, 3043, 3145, 3146, 3158, 4031, 5786, 5982, 6205, 6325, 6477, 7349, 8209, 8307, 8392, 8700, 8987, 8990, 9096, 9585–9591, 10,097, 10,777; A. E. 774, 836, 900, 1150, 1151; T. C. R. 74, 105, 371, 383, 455, 463–508, 580.]

CHAPTER XV.

CONCERNING MERIT.

When ye shall have done all those things which are commanded you, say, We are UNPROFITABLE SERVANTS: we have done that which was OUR DUTY TO DO. Luke xvii. 10.

FROM THE NEW JERUSALEM AND ITS HEAVENLY DOCTRINE, BY EMANUEL SWEDENBORG.

THEY who do goods that they may merit, do not do goods from the love of good, but from the love of reward; for he that wishes to merit, wishes to be rewarded. They who do thus, look for and place delight in the reward, and not in good: wherefore they are not spiritual, but natural.

2. To do good which is good, it must be from the love of good, thus for the sake of good. They who are in that love, do not wish to hear of merit; for they love to do, and perceive satisfaction in it: and on the other hand, they are saddened, if it is believed that it was done for the sake of anything of self. These things present themselves nearly like those who do good to their friends for the sake of friendship, to a brother for the sake of brotherhood, to wife and

children for the sake of wife and children, to their country for their country's sake, thus from friendship and love. They who think well also say and persuade that they do not do good for the sake of themselves, but for the sake of others.

3. THEY who do good for the sake of reward, do not do good from the LORD, but from themselves: for they regard themselves primarily, because they regard their own good; and the good of the neighbor, which is the good of a fellow-citizen, of human society, of one's country, of the church, they do not regard, except as a means to an end. Hence it is, that in the good of merit lurks the good of the love of self and the world; and this good is from man, and not from the LORD: and all good which is from man is not good; yea, as far as self and the world lurk in it, it is evil.

4. GENUINE charity and genuine faith are without all merit; for the delight of charity is good itself, and the delight of faith is truth itself: wherefore they who are in that charity and faith know what good not meritorious is, but not they who are not in charity and faith.

5. THAT good is not to be done for the sake of reward, the LORD Himself teaches in Luke: "If ye love them that love you, what grace have ye? for sinners do the same: rather, love your enemies, and do good, and lend, hoping for nothing: then shall your reward be great, and ye shall be the sons of the HIGHEST." vi. 32–35. That man cannot make good from himself to be good, the LORD also teaches in

John: "A man cannot take anything, unless it be given to him from heaven," iii. 27: and again: "JESUS said, I am the vine, ye the branches: as the branch cannot bear fruit of itself, unless it remain in the vine, so neither ye, unless ye remain in ME. He that remaineth in ME, and I in him, beareth much fruit; for, without ME, ye cannot do anything." xv. 4, 5.

6. SINCE all good and truth are from the LORD, and nothing from man; and since good from man is not good; it follows that no man has merit, but the LORD alone. The LORD's merit is, that from His proper power He saved the human race, and also that He saves them that do good from Him. It is hence that in the WORD he is called just, to whom the LORD's merit and justice are imputed; and he unjust, to whom his own justice and self-merit are imputed.

7. THE delight itself which there is in the love of doing good without the end of remuneration is the reward which remains forever; for, into that good are insinuated heaven and eternal happiness by the LORD.

8. TO think and believe that they who do good come into heaven, and also that good must be done that we may come into heaven, is not to regard reward as an end, thus neither to place merit in works; for those also who do good from the LORD think and believe that. But they who thus think, believe, and do, and are not in the love of good for the sake of good, do regard reward as an end, and place merit in works. H. D. 150–157. [For Ref. see p. 216.]

CHAPTER XVI.

CONCERNING REPENTANCE AND THE REMISSION OF SINS.

That REPENTANCE AND REMISSION OF SINS should be preached in His name among all nations. Luke xxiv. 47.

FROM THE NEW JERUSALEM AND ITS HEAVENLY DOCTRINE, BY EMANUEL SWEDENBORG.

HE who wishes to be saved, must confess his sins, and do repentance.

2. *To confess sins* is, to know one's evils, to see them in himself, to acknowledge them, to make himself guilty, and to condemn himself on account of them. When this is done before GOD, it is confessing sins.

3. *To do repentance* is, — after one has thus confessed his sins, and has supplicated for remission from an humble heart, — to desist from them, and to lead a new life according to the precepts of charity and faith.

4. HE who only acknowledges generally that he is a sinner, and makes himself guilty of all evils, and does not explore himself, that is, see his sins, — he makes confession, but not the confession of repentance. He,

because he does not know his evils, lives afterwards as before.

5. He who lives a life of charity and faith, does repentance daily, reflects upon the evils that are in him, acknowledges them, guards against them, supplicates the Lord for help: for man of himself continually falls; but he is continually raised up by the Lord, and is led to good. Such is the state of those who are in good. But they that are in evil fall continually, and are also continually lifted up by the Lord; but are only withdrawn, lest they should fall into the gravest evils; to which of themselves they tend with all effort.

6. A man who explores himself that he may do repentance, must explore his thoughts and the intentions of his will, and what he would do there if he were permitted; that is, if he did not fear the laws, and the loss of reputation, of honor, and of gain. There man's evils are: the evils which a man does with the body are all thence. They who do not explore the evils of their thought and will, cannot do repentance; for they think and will afterwards as before: and yet to will evils is to do them. This is exploring one's self.

7. Repentance of the mouth, and not of the life, is not repentance. By repentance of the mouth sins are not remitted, but by repentance of the life. Sins are continually remitted to man by the Lord, for He is mercy itself. But sins adhere to the man, however he supposes that they are remitted; nor are they removed from him, except by a life according to the precepts of

true faith. As far as he lives according to these, so far are sins removed; and as far as they are removed, so far they are remitted.

8. It is believed that sins, when they are remitted, are wiped away, or are washed off, as they do filth with water. But sins are not wiped away, but removed; that is, man is withheld from them, when he is kept in good by the Lord. And when he is kept in good, it appears as if he were without them; thus as if they were wiped away: and a man can so far be kept in good, as he is reformed. How man is reformed will be told in the following doctrine concerning Regeneration. He who believes that sins are remitted otherwise, is much deceived.

9. The signs that sins are remitted, that is, removed, are those which follow. They perceive a delight in worshipping God for the sake of God, and in serving the neighbor for the sake of the neighbor; thus in doing good for the sake of good, and in speaking truth for the sake of truth: they are unwilling to merit by anything of charity and faith: they shun and loathe evils; such as enmities, hatreds, revenges, adulteries, and the very thoughts of such things with intention. But the signs that sins are not remitted, that is, removed, are these which follow. They worship God not for the sake of God, and serve the neighbor not for the sake of the neighbor; thus they do not do good and speak truth for the sake of good and truth, but for the sake of self and the world: they wish to merit by their deeds: they

perceive no undelight in evils; as in enmity, in hatred, in revenge, in adulteries: and from them they think concerning them with all licentiousness.

10. The repentance which takes place in a free state is availing; but that which takes place in a state of compulsion is not availing. States of compulsion are states of disease, states of dejected mind from misfortune, states of imminent death; also every state of fear which takes away the use of reason. He who is evil, and in a state of compulsion promises repentance, and also does good, when he comes into a free state, returns into his former life. Not so the good.

11. After a man has explored himself, and acknowledged his sins, and done repentance, he must remain constant in good even to the end of life. For if he afterwards relapses into his former life of evil, and embraces it, he then commits profanation; for he then conjoins evil to good. Hence his latter state becomes worse than the former, according to the Lord's words: "When the unclean spirit has gone out of a man, it walketh through dry places, seeking rest, but doth not find: then it saith, I will return into my house whence I came out; and when it is come, it findeth it empty, and swept, and furnished: then it goeth, and adjoineth to itself seven other spirits worse than itself; and entering in, they dwell there: and the last things of that man become worse than the first." Matt. xii. 43–45. What profanation is may be seen in what follows. H. D. 159–169. [For Ref. see p. 216.]

CHAPTER XVII.

CONCERNING REGENERATION.

JESUS said, Verily, verily, I say unto thee, Except one be BORN AGAIN, he cannot see the kingdom of GOD. Except one BE BORN OF WATER AND OF THE SPIRIT, he cannot enter into the kingdom of GOD. That which is born of the flesh, is flesh; and that which is BORN OF THE SPIRIT, IS SPIRIT. Marvel not that I said unto thee, ye must be BORN AGAIN. The wind bloweth where it listeth; and thou hearest the sound thereof, but knowest not whence it cometh, and whither it goeth: so is every one that is BORN OF THE SPIRIT. John iii. 3–8.

FROM THE NEW JERUSALEM AND ITS HEAVENLY DOCTRINE, BY EMANUEL SWEDENBORG.

HE who does not receive spiritual life, that is, who is not generated anew by the LORD, cannot come into heaven; which the LORD teaches in John: "Verily, verily, I say unto you, except one be generated again, he cannot see the kingdom of GOD." iii. 3.

2. OF his parents man is not born into spiritual

life, but into natural life. Spiritual life is, to love God above all things, and to love the neighbor as one's self; and this according to the precepts of faith which the Lord has taught in the Word. But natural life is, to love one's self and the world above the neighbor, yea, above God Himself.

3. Every man is born of his parents into the evils of the love of self and the world. Every evil which by habit had as it were contracted a nature, is derived into the offspring, thus successively from parents, grandparents, and great-grandparents, in a long series back. Hence the derivation of evil at length becomes so great, that the all of a man's proper life is nothing but evil. This continual derivation is not broken and altered, except by a life of faith and charity from the Lord.

4. That which man derives hereditarily, he continually inclines to, and relapses into. He hence confirms that evil with himself, and also from himself superadds more. These evils are altogether contrary to spiritual life; they destroy it. On which account, unless a man receives from the Lord a new life, which is spiritual life, thus unless he is conceived anew, is born anew, and is brought up anew, that is, is created anew, he is damned: for he wills nothing else, and thence thinks nothing else, but what is of self and the world; like as they do in hell.

5. No one can be regenerated, unless he knows such things as are of the new life; that is, such as

are of spiritual life. The things which are of the new life, or which are of spiritual life, are the truths which are to be believed and the goods which are to be done: the former are of faith, the latter of charity. These things no one can know from himself; for man apprehends only the things that have been obvious to the senses. From these he procures a lume [light] to himself, which lume is called natural, from which he sees nothing else but the things that are of the world and those that are of self; but not those that are of heaven and those that are of GOD. The latter he learns from revelation: as, that the LORD, who is GOD from eternity, came into the world to save the human race: that He has all power in heaven and in earth: that the all of faith and the all of charity, thus all truth and good, are from Him: that there is a heaven and a hell: that man is to live to eternity,—in heaven, if he has done well; if ill, in hell.

6. THESE and more are the things of faith, which a man who is to be regenerated ought to know: for he who knows them can think them, then will them, and at length do them, and so have new life. While he who does not know that the LORD is the Savior of the human race, cannot have faith in Him, love Him, and so do good for His sake. He who does not know that all good is from Him, cannot think that his salvation is from Him; still less can he will that it should be so; thus cannot live from Him. He who

does not know that there is a hell and that there is a heaven, nor that there is eternal life, cannot even think about the life of heaven, nor apply himself to receiving it. And so in other cases.

7. EVERY one has an internal man and an external man. It is the internal which is called the spiritual man, and the external the natural man. Both must be regenerated, that the man may be regenerated. With the man who is not regenerated, the external or natural man rules, and the internal serves; but with the man who is regenerated, the internal or spiritual man rules, and the external serves. Whence it is manifest, that with man from nativity the order of life is inverted; namely, that which ought to rule, serves; and that which ought to serve, rules. This order must be inverted, that the man may be saved; and this inversion can in no way take place, but by regeneration from the LORD.

8. WHAT it is for the internal man to rule and the external to serve, and the reverse, may be illustrated by this. If a man places all good in pleasure, in gain, and in pride, and takes delight in hatred and revenge, and interiorly in himself studies out reasons which confirm; then the external man rules, and the internal serves. But when a man perceives good and delight in thinking and willing well, sincerely, and justly, and in outwardly speaking and doing in like manner; then the internal man rules, and the external serves.

9. THE internal man is first regenerated by the

LORD, and afterwards the external; and the latter through the former: for the internal man is regenerated by thinking those things which are of faith and charity; but the external, by a life according to them. This is understood by the LORD's words: "Except one be born of water and of the Spirit, he cannot enter into the kingdom of GOD." John iii. 5. Water in the spiritual sense is the truth of faith, and the Spirit is a life according to it.

10. THE man who is regenerated, is, as to his internal man, in heaven, and is an angel there with the angels; among whom he also comes after death. He can then live the life of heaven,—love the LORD, love the neighbor, understand truth, be wise in good, and perceive blessedness therefrom. H. D. 173–182.

[See also, A. C. 868, 911, 913, 935, 936, 1555, 1740, 1937, 2063, 2189, 2657, 2678, 2679, 2682, 2689, 2694, 2701, 2704, 2877, 2878, 2979, 3043, 3089, 3138, 3145, 3146, 3167, 3179, 3203, 3212, 3286, 3310, 3318, 3539, 3576, 3584, 3603, 3610, 3665, 3696, 3701, 3761. 3868, 3870, 3876, 3877, 3882, 3913, 4096, 4104, 4110, 4111, 4136, 4248, 4353, 4538, 4564, 5122, 5128, 5280, 8548–8553, 8635–8640, 8725, 8742–8747, 8987, 8991, 10,360, 10,367; A. E. 178, 434, 650, 710, 724; A. R. 84, 85, 224, 463, 510, 798, 815, 832; T. C. R. 571–625.]

CHAPTER XVIII.

CONCERNING TEMPTATION.

JESUS was led by the Spirit into the wilderness, being forty days TEMPTED OF THE DEVIL. Luke iv. 1, 2.

Lead us not into TEMPTATION. Matt. vi. 13.

Watch and pray, that ye enter not into TEMPTATION. Matt. xxvi. 41.

Because thou hast kept the WORD of My patience, I also will KEEP THEE FROM the HOUR OF TEMPTATION. Rev. iii. 10.

FROM THE NEW JERUSALEM AND ITS HEAVENLY DOCTRINE, BY EMANUEL SWEDENBORG.

THEY only who are being regenerated undergo Spiritual Temptations: for spiritual temptations are pains of the mind with those who are in goods and truths, induced by evil spirits. While the latter are exciting the evils that are with the former, there arises an anxiety, which is of temptation. Man knows not whence it comes, because he is not acquainted with this its origin.

2. FOR there are with every man evil spirits and

good spirits: the evil spirits are in his evils, and the good spirits in his goods. When evil spirits come near, they draw forth his evils; and the good spirits, on the other hand, his goods. Thence is collision and combat; from which the man has interior anxiety, which is temptation. It is hence manifest, that temptations are induced by hell, and not out of heaven: which is also according to the faith of the church; which is, that GOD tempts no one.

3. THERE are also interior anxieties with those who are not in goods and truths; but natural anxieties, and not spiritual. They are known apart by this, — that natural anxieties have worldly things for their object; but spiritual anxieties, heavenly things.

4. IN temptations the dominion of good over evil, or of evil over good, is contended for. The evil, which wishes to rule, is in the natural or external man; and the good, in the spiritual or internal. If evil conquers, then the natural man rules; but the spiritual man, if good conquers.

5. THESE combats are carried on by means of the truths of faith which are from the WORD. From these must the man fight against evils and falsities: if from other things than these, he does not conquer; because the LORD is not in other things. Since the combat is carried on by the truths of faith, for that reason a man is not admitted into that combat before he is in the knowledges of truth and good, and has acquired some spiritual life therefrom. On which

account these combats do not exist with a man, until he has become of adult age.

6. If the man yields, his state after temptation becomes worse than his state before it; because evil has then acquired to itself power over good, and falsity over truth.

7. Since faith is rare at this day, because there is not charity, — for the church is at its end, — on that account few at this day are admitted into any spiritual temptations. Hence it is, that it is scarcely known what they are, and to what they conduce.

8. Temptations conduce to acquiring dominion to good over evil, and to truth over falsity; also, to the confirming of truths, and to conjoining them to goods; and at the same time to shaking off evils and thence falsities. They conduce also to opening the spiritual internal man, and to subjecting to it the natural; so, also, to breaking up the loves of self and the world, and to subduing the concupiscences which are thence. Which things being done, there comes to man illustration and perception as to what truth and good are, and what falsity and evil are. Thence there comes to man understanding and wisdom, which afterwards increase from day to day.

9. The Lord alone fights for man in temptations. If a man does not believe that the Lord alone fights for him and conquers for him, he is then undergoing only external temptation, which is not beneficial to him. H. D. 187–195. [For Ref. see p. 216.]

CHAPTER XIX.

CONCERNING DEATH AND THE RESURRECTION.

Now that the dead ARE RAISED, even Moses showed at the bush, when he calleth the LORD the GOD of Abraham, and the GOD of Isaac, and the GOD of Jacob. For He is not a GOD of the dead, but of the LIVING: for ALL, to Him, ARE LIVING. Luke xx. 37, 38.

JESUS said, I am the RESURRECTION and the LIFE. He that believeth in ME, though he have died, yet SHALL HE LIVE. John xi. 25.

FROM THE NEW JERUSALEM AND ITS HEAVENLY DOCTRINE, BY EMANUEL SWEDENBORG.

MAN was so created that as to his internal he cannot die; for, he can believe in GOD, and also love GOD, and thus be conjoined to GOD by faith and love: and to be conjoined to GOD is to live to eternity.

2. THIS internal is with every man who is born: his external is that by which he effects those things which are of faith and love. It is the internal which is called the spirit, and the external which is called the

body. The external, which is called the body, is accommodated to uses in the natural world: this is rejected, when man dies. But the internal, which is called the spirit, is accommodated to uses in the spiritual world: this does not die. This internal is then a good spirit and an angel, if the man had been good in the world; but an evil spirit, if the man in the world had been evil.

3. The spirit of a man, after the death of the body, appears in the spiritual world in the human form, altogether as in the world. He enjoys also the faculty of seeing, hearing, speaking, and feeling, as in the world; and he exercises every faculty of thinking, willing, and doing, as in the world: in a word, he is a man as to each and every thing; except that he is not encompassed by that gross body with which he was in the world. He leaves that when he dies; nor does he ever resume it.

4. It is this continuation of life, which is understood by the resurrection. The reason why men believe that they are not to rise again before the last judgment, when also every visible thing of the world is to perish, is because they have not understood the Word; also, because sensual men place life in the body, and believe that unless this were to live again, all would be over with man.

5. The life of man after death is the life of his love and the life of his faith: hence, as his love and as his faith had been when he lived in the world, such life

remains to him forever. It is the life of hell to those that have loved themselves and the world above all things, and the life of heaven to those who have loved God above all things, and the neighbor as themselves: the latter are they who have faith; but the former are they that do not have faith. It is the life of heaven, which is called eternal life; and it is the life of hell, which is called spiritual death.

6. The Word teaches that man lives after death; as, that God is not the God of the dead, but of the living, Matt. xxii. 32: That Lazarus after death was taken up into heaven, but the rich man cast into hell, Luke xvi. 22, 23; and further, That Abraham, Isaac, and Jacob are there, Matt. viii. 11; xxii. 31, 32; Luke xx. 37, 38: That Jesus said to the thief, To-day thou shalt be with me in paradise, Luke xxiii. 43. — H. D. 223–228.

FROM THE WORK ON HEAVEN AND HELL, BY EMANUEL SWEDENBORG.

7. When the body is no longer able to perform its functions in the natural world, corresponding to the thoughts and affections of its spirit which it has from the spiritual world, the man is then said to die. This takes place when the respiratory motions of the lungs and the systolic motions of the heart cease. But still the man does not die, but is only separated from the corporeal part which he had for use in the world; for the man himself lives. It is said that the man himself lives, because man is not man from the body, but from the spirit: since the spirit thinks in man; and thought

with affection makes man. It is hence manifest, that man, when he dies, only passes from one world into another. Hence it is, that death, in the WORD, in its internal sense, signifies resurrection and continuation of life. H. H. 445.

FROM THE HEAVENLY ARCANA, BY EMANUEL SWEDENBORG.

8. MOST at this day, who are of the church, believe that every one is to rise again at the last day, and then with the body; which opinion is so universal, that scarce any one from doctrine believes otherwise. But this opinion has prevailed on this account, because the natural man supposes that the body alone is what lives; wherefore, unless he should believe that that was to receive life anew, he would altogether deny a resurrection. But the reality is this: Man immediately after death rises again, and then appears to himself in a body altogether as in the world; with such a face, with such members, arms, hands, feet, breast, belly, loins: yea, also, when he sees himself and touches himself, he says that he is a man as in the world. But still, it is not his external which he carried about in the world, that he sees and touches; but it is the internal, which constitutes that very human which lives, and which had the external around itself, or outside of the particulars of itself; by which it could be in the world, and act conveniently there, and discharge functions. The earthly corporeal itself is no longer of any use to it: it is in another world, where are other functions, and other forces and powers; to which its body, such as it

has there, is adapted. This it sees with its eyes, — not with those which it had in the world, but with those which it has there; which are those of its internal man, and out of which, through the eyes of the body, it had before seen worldly and earthly things. It feels it also by the touch, — not with the hands, or the sense of touch, which it enjoyed in the world; but with the hands and the sense of touch which it enjoys there. Every sense also is more exquisite and more perfect there, because it is that of the internal man released from the external: for the internal is in a more perfect state, because it gives to the external to exercise the senses; but when it acts into the external, as in the world, the sensation is then blunted and obscured. Besides, it is the internal which feels the internal, and the external which feels the external. Hence it is, that men after death see each other, and are in society together according to the interiors. A. C. 5078.

[See A. C. 70, 168–189, 314–323, 443–448, 2119, 3957, 4527, 5078, 5079, 8939, 10,591–10,597, 10,758; A. R. 153; H. H. 445–460.]

CHAPTER XX.

CONCERNING THE WORLD OF SPIRITS.

Abraham in heaven, said to the rich man in hell, Between us and you a GREAT CHASM IS FIXED. Luke xvi. 26. — T. C. R. 455.

FROM THE WORK ON HEAVEN AND HELL, BY EMANUEL SWEDENBORG.

THE World of Spirits is not heaven, nor is it hell; but it is a middle place or state between both: for thither man first comes after death; and then, after a time required, according to his life in the world, he is either elevated into heaven, or cast into hell.

2. THE World of Spirits is a middle place between heaven and hell; and it is also a middle state of man after death. That it is a middle place, was manifest to me from this, — that the hells are beneath, and the heavens above: and that it is a middle state, from this, — that man, as long as he is there, is not yet in heaven, nor in hell.

3. ALMOST every man at this day is in such a state, that he knows truths, and from science and

also from understanding thinks them, and either makes much of them, or little of them, or nothing of them, or does contrary to them from the love of evil and thence the faith of falsity: therefore, that either heaven or hell may be for him, he is after death first brought into the World of Spirits; and there a conjunction of good and truth is made with those who are to be elevated into heaven, and a conjunction of evil and falsity with those who are to be cast into hell. For it is not permitted to any one, in heaven nor in hell, to have the mind divided; that is, to understand one thing and to will another: but what he wills, he must understand; and what he understands, he must will. Wherefore, in heaven, he who wills good must understand truth; and in hell, he who wills evil must understand falsity: therefore, with the good, falsities are there removed, and truths are given agreeable and conformable to their good; and with the evil, truths are there removed, and falsities are given agreeable and conformable to their evil. From these things it is manifest what the World of Spirits is.

4. In the World of Spirits there is a vast number; because the first meeting of all is there: and all are there explored and prepared. There is no fixed term for their continuance there: some only enter it, and are soon either taken away into heaven, or cast down into hell: some remain there only for a few weeks; some for several years; but not beyond thirty. The

varieties of continuance exist from the correspondence and the want of correspondence of the interiors and exteriors with man.

5. MEN after death, as soon as they come into the World of Spirits, are well distinguished by the LORD: the evil are immediately bound to the infernal society in which they were in the world as to their ruling love; and the good are immediately bound to the heavenly society in which they also were in the world as to love, charity, and faith. But although they are thus distinguished, still they who have been friends and acquaintances in the life of the body, all meet together in that world, and converse one with another, when they desire it; especially wives and husbands, and also brothers and sisters. H. H. 421, 422, 425, 426, 427.

FROM THE TRUE CHRISTIAN RELIGION OF EMANUEL SWEDENBORG.

6. SINCE the delights of hell are opposite to the delights of heaven, there is a great Interspace between them, into which from above flow in the delights of heaven, and from beneath the delights of hell. It is this Interspace which is meant by the *great chasm fixed* between those who are in heaven and those who are in hell. Luke xvi. 26. — T. C. R. 455.

[See H. H. 421–535; A. C. 320–323, 443–448, 5846–5866, 5976–5993; C. L. 1–26, 115; T. C. R. 160, 281, 459, 475–478, 506, 568, 570, 622; A. R. 843, 850, 856, 857, 884, 886.]

CHAPTER XXI.

CONCERNING THE JUDGMENT.

The WORD which I have spoken, THAT SHALL JUDGE HIM in the last day. John xii. 48.

And I saw the dead, small and great, stand before GOD; and the BOOKS were opened: and another BOOK was opened, which is the BOOK OF LIFE: and the dead WERE JUDGED out of the things WRITTEN IN THE BOOKS, ACCORDING TO THEIR WORKS. Rev. xx. 12.

He that is UNJUST, let him be UNJUST STILL; and he that is FILTHY, let him be FILTHY STILL: and he that is RIGHTEOUS, let him be RIGHTEOUS STILL; and he that is HOLY, let him be HOLY STILL. Apoc. xxii. 11.

THE JUDGMENT OF EVERY ONE AFTER DEATH.

FROM THE HEAVENLY ARCANA OF EMANUEL SWEDENBORG.

EVERY man has two memories; the one exterior, the other interior: and the exterior is proper to his body, but the interior proper to his spirit.

2. THE interior memory is such, that there are inscribed in it all the particular things, yea, the most particular, which the man has ever thought, spoken, and

done, yea, which have appeared to him as a shade, with the most minute points, from earliest infancy to the last of old age. Of all these things man has the memory with him when he comes into the other life, and is gradually brought into all recollection of them. This is the BOOK OF HIS LIFE ; which is opened in the other life, and according to which he is judged. This, man can scarce believe; but still it is most true. All his ends which were to him in obscurity, also all things thought and all things spoken and done therefrom, to the smallest point of them all, are in that Book, that is, in the interior memory ; and, as often as the LORD grants, they are manifest before the angels, as in clear day. A. C. 2469, 2474.

FROM THE WORK ON HEAVEN AND HELL, BY EMANUEL SWEDENBORG.

3. WHEN man enters into the other life, he is first received by angels ; who perform for him all good offices, and also converse with him concerning the LORD, concerning heaven, concerning angelic life, and instruct him in truths and goods.

But if the man, then a spirit, is such that he had indeed known like things in the world, but in heart denied or despised them, he then, after some conversation, desires and also seeks to depart from them. When the angels perceive this, they leave him ; and he, after some consociations with others, is at length associated with those who are in like evil with himself. When this is effected, he turns himself away from the LORD, and turns his face to the hell with which he had been conjoined in the world; where are those who are in a like love of evil. From these things it is manifest that the LORD draws away every spirit to Himself by the angels, and also by influx from heaven; but that the spirits who are in evil altogether resist, and as it were tear themselves away from the LORD, and are drawn by their evil as by a rope, thus by hell: and inasmuch as they are drawn, and by reason of the love of evil are willing to follow, it is evident that from freedom they cast themselves into hell.

4. [As to good] spirits, after they have by instructions been prepared for heaven, — which is effected in a short time, for the reason that they are in spiritual ideas, which comprehend many things together, — they are then clothed with angelic garments, which for the most part are white, as of fine linen; and thus they are brought to a way which tends upwards to heaven, and are delivered to the angel-guards there, and are then received by other angels, and are introduced into societies, and into many gratifications there. Every one is next brought into his society by the LORD; which also is done through various ways, sometimes by winding paths: the ways by which they are led no angel knows, but the LORD alone. When they come to their society, their interiors are then opened; and since these are conformable to the interiors of the angels who are in that society, they are on that account immediately acknowledged, and received with joy. H. H. 548, 519. [See also, H. H. 461–484, 491–520, 545–550.]

THE LAST OR GENERAL JUDGMENT.

FROM THE APOCALYPSE REVEALED OF EMANUEL SWEDENBORG.

FROM the time when the LORD was in the world, when he performed a Last Judgment in person, (John xii. 31; xvi. 11; Luke x. 18,) it was permitted that they who were in civil and moral good, although in no spiritual good, — whence in externals they appeared like Christians, but in internals were devils, — should remain longer than the rest in the World of Spirits, which is in the midst between heaven and hell. And it was at length granted them to make to themselves fixed habitations there; and also, by the abuse of correspondences and by fantasies, to form as it were heavens to themselves: which they also formed in great abundance. But when they were multiplied to such abundance that they intercepted the spiritual light and spiritual heat between the superior heavens and man on earth, the LORD then passed a Last Judgment, and dissipated those imaginary heavens; which was done in this manner: the externals, by which they counterfeited Christians, were taken away; and the internals, in which they were devils, were opened: and then they were seen to be such as they were in themselves; and those who were seen to be devils were cast into hell, each according to the evils of his life. This was done in 1757. A. R. 865.

[See L. J., & C. L. J., also A. R. and A. E. throughout.]

CHAPTER XXII.

CONCERNING THE STATE OF INFANTS IN THE OTHER LIFE.

I say unto you, that THEIR ANGELS IN THE HEAVENS do always behold the face of My FATHER who is in the heavens. Matt. xviii. 10.

JESUS said, Suffer the LITTLE CHILDREN to come unto ME, and forbid them not: for OF SUCH is the kingdom of GOD. Mark x. 14.

FROM THE WORK ON HEAVEN AND HELL, BY EMANUEL SWEDENBORG.

IT is the belief of some, that only the Infants who were born within the church come into heaven; but not those without the church. The reason they give is, that infants within the church were baptized, and were by baptism initiated into the faith of the church. But they do not know that no one has heaven or faith by baptism: for baptism is only for a sign and memorial that man is to be regenerated; and that he can be regenerated who is born within the church: since there the WORD is, wherein are the divine truths by which regeneration is effected; and there the LORD is known, from whom regeneration is. Let them know, therefore, that every infant, wherever he was born, whether within the church or out of it, whether of pious or of unpious parents, is, when he dies, received by the LORD, and is brought up in heaven, and according to divine order is taught and imbued with the affections of good, and through them with the knowledges of truth; and afterwards, as he is perfected in intelligence and wisdom, is introduced into heaven, and becomes an angel. Every one who thinks from reason may know that no one is born for hell, but all for heaven; and that the man himself is in fault, if he comes into hell: but that infants can as yet be in no fault.

2. INFANTS who die, are equally infants in the other life. They have a like infantile mind, a like innocence in ignorance, and a like tenderness in all things. They are only the first beginnings of the capacity of becoming angels: for infants are not angels, but become angels. For every one who departs out of the world, is in a like state of his life: an infant, in the state of an infant; a child, in the state of a child; a youth, a man, an old man, in the state of a youth, of a man, and of an old man. But the state of every one is afterwards changed. Yet the state of infants exceeds the state of the others in this: that they are in innocence, and that evil from actual life is not yet rooted in them. And innocence is such, that all

things of heaven may be implanted in it; since innocence is the receptacle of the truth of faith and of the good of love.

3. THE state of infants in the other life is much better than the state of infants in the world; for they are not clothed with an earthly body, but with a like one as the angels. The earthly body is in itself heavy: it does not receive its first sensations and first movements from the inner or spiritual world, but from the outer or natural world. Wherefore infants in the world must learn to walk, to move the limbs, and to speak: yea, the senses, as seeing and hearing, must be opened by use. It is otherwise with infants in the other life. Because they are spirits, they act immediately according to their interiors: they walk without practice; they speak also, but at first from general affections not yet so distinguished into ideas of thoughts. Yet shortly they are initiated into these also, and this because their exteriors are homogeneous with their interiors.

4. INFANTS, as soon as they are raised up, which takes place immediately after death, are carried away into heaven, and delivered to angels who are of the female sex, who in the life of their body tenderly loved infants, and at the same time loved GOD. These, because in the world they loved all infants from a kind of maternal tenderness, receive them as their own; and the infants also, from an implanted disposition, love them as their own mothers. There

are as many infants with each one, as she desires from a spiritual parental affection.

5. INFANTS do not immediately after death come into the angelic state, but are gradually introduced by the knowledges of good and truth, and this according to all heavenly order; for the least of all the things of their disposition are known to the LORD: wherefore, according to all and each of the movements of their inclination, they are led to receive the truths of good and the goods of truth.

6. MANY may suppose that infants remain infants in heaven, and that they are as infants among the angels. They who are in ignorance as to what an angel is, may have been confirmed in this opinion from the images here and there in temples; where angels are exhibited as infants. But the reality is altogether otherwise. Intelligence and wisdom make an angel; and as long as infants do not yet have these, they are indeed with the angels, but are not angels. But when they are intelligent and wise, they then first become angels: yea, what I have wondered at, they then do not appear as infants, but as adults; for they are then no longer of an infantile, but of a more adult angelic genius. This do intelligence and wisdom bring with them.

7. WHAT the difference is between those who die infants and those who die adults shall also be told. They who die adults have a plane acquired from the earthly and material world; and they take it with

them. This plane is their memory and its natural corporeal affection. This remains fixed, and is then quiescent: but still it serves their thought as an ultimate plane after death; for the thought flows into it. Hence it is, that such as that plane is, and such as is the correspondence of the rational with the things that are therein, such after death is the man. But infants who died infants, and have been brought up in heaven, have not such a plane, but a spiritual-natural plane; since they derive nothing from the material world and the earthly body: on which account they cannot be in so gross affections and thence thoughts; for they derive all things from heaven. Besides, infants are ignorant that they were born in the world; wherefore they believe that they were born in heaven. Whence they do not know what any other nativity is but a spiritual one; which is effected by the knowledges of good and truth, and by intelligence and wisdom; from which man is man. Because these are from the LORD, they believe that they are the LORD'S Himself, and love to have it so. But still, the state of men who grow up on the earth may become equally as perfect as the state of the infants who are in heaven, if they remove corporeal and earthly loves, which are the loves of self and the world, and in their place receive spiritual loves. H. H. 329, 330, 331, 332, 336, 340, 345. [See also H. H. 329–345, and A. C. 2289–2309.]

CHAPTER XXIII.

CONCERNING THE GENTILES, OR HEATHEN, IN THE OTHER LIFE.

I beheld, and, lo, a GREAT MULTITUDE, which no one could number, of ALL NATIONS, and TRIBES, and PEOPLES, and TONGUES, stood before the throne, and before the LAMB, clothed with white robes, and palms in their hands. Rev. vii. 9.

FROM THE WORK ON HEAVEN AND HELL, BY EMANUEL SWEDENBORG.

IT is a common opinion, that they who were born out of the church, who are called heathen, or Gentiles, cannot be saved, for the reason that they have not the WORD, and are thus ignorant of the LORD; and without the LORD there is no salvation. But still, that they also are saved may be known from this alone, that the LORD's mercy is universal, that is, towards every one; since they are born men equally as those that are within the church, who are few in comparison; and since it is not their fault that they are ignorant of the LORD. Every one who thinks from any enlightened reason can see that no man was born for hell: for the LORD is love itself; and His love is to will to save all. Wherefore also He provides that all may have a religion, and through it an acknowledgment of a Divine, and interior life; since to live according to a religion is to live interiorly: for then one regards a Divine; and as far as he regards this, so far he does not regard the world; but removes himself from the world, thus from the life of the world, which is exterior life.

2. THAT the Gentiles are saved equally as Christians, those may know, who know what makes heaven with man: for heaven is in man; and they who have heaven in themselves come into heaven. Heaven in a man is to acknowledge a Divine, and to be led by the Divine. It is the first and primary thing of every religion to acknowledge a Divine; a religion which does not ac-acknowledge a Divine is not religion: and the precepts of every religion look to worship, thus to how the Divine is to be worshipped, that one may be acceptable to Him; and when this is seated in one's mind, thus as far as he wills it, or as far as he loves it, so far he is led by the LORD. It is known that the Gentiles live a moral life equally as Christians, and many of them a better one than Christians.

3. THE Gentiles who have led a moral life, and lived in obedience and subordination, and in mutual charity according to their religion, and have thence received something of conscience, are accepted in the other life, and are there instructed with diligent care by the angels in the goods and truths of faith; and while they are instructed they behave themselves modestly, intelligently, and wisely, and easily receive the truths, and

are imbued with them. Against the truths of faith also they have formed to themselves no principles of falsity, which are to be shaken off; still less scandals against the LORD; as many Christians have, who cherish no other idea concerning Him than as of an ordinary man. It is otherwise with the Gentiles, who, when they hear that GOD became Man, and thus manifested Himself in the world, acknowledge it forthwith, and adore the LORD; saying that GOD manifested Himself wholly because He is the GOD of heaven and earth, and because the human race is His. It is a divine truth, that without the LORD there is no salvation; but this is to be understood thus: that there is no salvation but from the LORD. There are in the universe many earths, and all full of inhabitants. Scarcely any there know that the LORD assumed the Humanity on our Earth. But still, because they adore a Divine under the human form, they are accepted and led by the LORD.

4. THE Church of the LORD is spread through the universal circle of lands; and all are in it who have lived in the good of charity according to their religion: and the Church where the WORD is, and by it the LORD is known, is to those who are out of the Church as the Heart and the Lungs in man; from which all the viscera and members of the body live, variously, according to their forms, situations, and connections. H. H. 318, 319, 321, 328. — [See H. H. 308; S. S. 104–113; A. C. 2589–2605; also E. U.]

CHAPTER XXIV.

CONCERNING HEAVEN AND HELL.

Treasure up for yourselves treasures in HEAVEN. Matt. vi. 20.

If thou wilt enter into LIFE, keep the Commandments. Matt. xix. 17.

And they shall come forth, they that have done good things, to the resurrection of LIFE; and they that have practised evil things, to the resurrection of JUDGMENT. John v. 29.

And in HELL he lifted up his eyes, being in TORMENTS. Luke xvi. 23.

FROM THE NEW JERUSALEM AND ITS HEAVENLY DOCTRINE, BY EMANUEL SWEDENBORG.

THERE are two things which make the life of man's spirit, Love and Faith, — love the life of his Will, and faith the life of his Understanding. The love of good, and thence the faith of truth, make the life of Heaven; and the love of evil, and thence the faith of falsity, make the life of Hell.

2. LOVE to the LORD and love towards the neigh-

bor make heaven: and so does faith; but the latter, only so far as it has life from those loves. And because both those loves, and the faith thence, are from the LORD, it is hence manifest that the LORD makes heaven.

3. HEAVEN is with every one according to the reception of love and faith from the LORD; and they who receive heaven from the LORD while they live in the world, come into heaven after death.

4. THEY who receive heaven from the LORD are they who have heaven in themselves; for heaven is in man: which also the LORD teaches: "They shall not say, Lo, the kingdom of GOD is here! or, lo there! for, behold, the kingdom of GOD is in you." Luke xvii. 21.

5. HEAVEN with man is in his internal, thus in willing and thinking from love and faith; and thence in the external, which is to do and speak from love and faith: but it is not in the external without the internal; for all hypocrites can do well and speak well, but not will well and think well.

6. WHEN a man comes into the other life, which takes place immediately after death, it is manifest whether heaven is in him; but not when he is living in the world: for in the world the external appears, and not the internal. But in the other life the internal is manifest; because man then lives as to his spirit.

7. ETERNAL happiness, which is also called heav-

enly joy, do those have who are in love to and faith in the LORD from the LORD: that love and that faith have in them that joy. Into it, after death, comes the man who has heaven in himself: meantime, it lies stored up in his internal. In the heavens there is a communion of all goods: the peace, the intelligence, the wisdom, and the happiness of all are communicated to every one there; but yet to each according to the reception of love and faith from the LORD. Hence it is manifest, how great the peace, the intelligence, the wisdom, and the happiness in heaven are.

8. IN the same way as love to the LORD and love towards the neighbor make the life of heaven with man, so the love of self and the love of the world, when they reign, make the life of hell with him; for these loves are opposite to those. On which account, they with whom the loves of self and the world reign can receive nothing from heaven; but the things which they receive are from hell: for, whatever a man loves, and whatever he believes, is either from heaven, or is from hell.

9. THEY with whom the love of self and the love of the world reign, do not know what heaven, and what the happiness of heaven are; and it appears incredible to them, that happiness is given in any other loves than those: when yet, the happiness of heaven so far enters, as those loves, as ends, are removed. The happiness which succeeds on their being

removed is so great, that it exceeds all comprehension of man.

10. MAN'S life cannot be changed after death: it then remains as it had been. For the entire spirit of man is such as his love is; and infernal love cannot be transcribed into heavenly love, since they are opposite. This is understood by the words of Abraham to the rich man in hell: "There is a great chasm between you and us, so that they who wish to pass to you cannot; neither also can they pass thence to us." Luke xvi. 26. It is hence manifest, that they who come into hell remain there to eternity; and that they who come into heaven remain there to eternity. H. D. 230–239.

CONTENTS OF EMANUEL SWEDENBORG'S WORK ON HEAVEN AND HELL.

HEAVEN.

THE WORLD OF SPIRITS.

HELL.

PART III.

INSTITUTES OF THE NEW CHURCH.

PART III.

INSTITUTES OF THE NEW CHURCH.

CHAPTER I.

CONCERNING THE CHURCH.

Where two or three are gathered together in My name, there am I in the midst of them. Matt. xviii. 20.

That they all may be one; as THOU, FATHER, art in ME, and I in THEE; that THEY also MAY BE ONE in us. John xvii. 21.

FROM THE NEW JERUSALEM AND ITS HEAVENLY DOCTRINE, BY EMANUEL SWEDENBORG.

THAT which makes heaven with man also makes the church; for, as love and faith make heaven, so also do love and faith make the church. Hence it may be manifest what the church is, from the things that were said before concerning heaven.

2. THAT is called the Church, where the LORD is acknowledged, and where the WORD is; for the essentials of the church are love to and faith in the LORD from the LORD: and the WORD teaches how a man

should live, that he may receive love and faith from the LORD.

3. THAT there may be a Church, there must be Doctrine from the WORD; since without doctrine the WORD is not understood. But doctrine alone does not make the church with a man, but a life according to it. It follows hence, that faith alone does not make the church; but a life of faith, which is charity. Genuine doctrine is the doctrine of charity, and at the same time of faith; and not the doctrine of faith without the former: for the doctrine of charity, and of faith at the same time, is the doctrine of life; but not the doctrine of faith without the doctrine of charity.

4. THEY who are without the Church, and acknowledge one GOD, and live according to their religion in a certain charity towards the neighbor, are in communion with those who are of the Church; since no one who believes in a GOD, and lives well, is damned. Hence it is manifest, that the LORD's church is everywhere in the universal world; although in particular it is where the LORD is acknowledged, and where the WORD is.

5. EVERY one in whom the church is, is saved; but every one in whom the church is not, is condemned. H. D. 241–245.

FROM THE APOCALYPSE EXPLAINED OF EMANUEL SWEDENBORG.

6. THE church is the heaven of the LORD on the earth; and in particular, the church is a man of the church, or a man in whom the church is: and a man who is a church, or in whom the church is, is a heaven

in the least form; for he corresponds to all things of heaven. A. E. 555.

FROM THE WORK ON DIVINE PROVIDENCE, BY EMANUEL SWEDENBORG.

7. THERE are Three Essentials of the church, — the acknowledgment of the LORD's Divinity, the acknowledgment of the Holiness of the WORD, and the life which is called Charity. According to the life which is Charity every man has faith; from the WORD he has a knowledge of what the life must be; and from the LORD he has reformation and salvation. D. P. 259.

FROM THE TRUE CHRISTIAN RELIGION OF EMANUEL SWEDENBORG.

8. THE order into which the church is restored by GOD is this: that GOD is in all and each of the things of it; and the neighbor is he towards whom order is to be exercised. The laws of that order are as many as there are truths in the WORD. The laws which regard GOD must make its head; the laws which regard the neighbor must make its body; and the ceremonies must make the dress: for, unless these should hold the others together in their order, it would be as if the body were made naked, and exposed to the heat in summer, and to the cold in winter; or as if the walls and roofs should be taken away from a temple, and so the shrine, the altar, and the pulpit should stand forth under the open sky, exposed to various violences. T. C. R. 55.

[See also, S. S. 76–79, 104–118; A. C. 637, 916, 931, 1100, 1795, 1799, 1834, 2385, 2853, 2982, 3445, 4766, 6637, 9276, 10,151, 10,452.]

CHAPTER II.

INTRODUCTION TO THE TWO SACRAMENTS.

THE LORD has given to the church the two representative Sacraments, BAPTISM, and the HOLY SUPPER; and in their spiritual sense they involve all that we have to do in preparation for heaven. Baptism represents the purification of the mind, and the removal of everything that is evil and false; and the Holy Supper represents the reception and implantation of what is good and true: thus the two Sacraments represent the whole work of regeneration, — the work of rejecting the influence of evil spirits, and of yielding to the influence of the LORD and his angels.

2. IT is made our duty to receive Baptism before we receive the Holy Supper, because the spiritual works which are represented by Baptism, precede those which are represented by the Holy Supper, and prepare the way for them; and in the degree that we resist and put away what is evil and false, in that degree we are able to receive what is good and true: or, in other words, in the degree that we perform the spiritual works represented by Baptism, in that degree we are prepared to receive the Holy Supper, and the things that are represented by it.

CONCERNING BAPTISM.

And JESUS came and spake unto them, saying, All power is given unto ME in heaven and upon earth. Go ye, therefore, and make disciples of all the nations, BAPTIZING THEM INTO THE NAME of the FATHER, and of the SON, and of the HOLY SPIRIT; teaching them to observe all things whatsoever I have commanded you: and lo, I am with you all the days, until the consummation of the age: Amen. Matt. xxviii. 18–20.

FROM THE NEW JERUSALEM AND ITS HEAVENLY DOCTRINE, BY EMANUEL SWEDENBORG.

BAPTISM was instituted for a sign that a man is from the church, and as a memorial that he must be regenerated: for the washing of Baptism is nothing else than spiritual washing, which is regeneration.

2. ALL regeneration is effected by the LORD, through the truths of faith, and by a life according to them. Baptism, therefore, testifies that the man is from the church, and that he can be regenerated. For in the church the LORD is acknowledged, who regenerates; and there the WORD is, wherein the truths are, through which is regeneration.

3. THIS the LORD teaches in John: "Except one be born of water and of the Spirit, he cannot enter into the kingdom of GOD." iii. 5. Water, in the spiritual sense, is truth of faith from the WORD; the Spirit is a life according to it; and to be born of them, is to be regenerated.

4. SINCE every one who is regenerated also undergoes temptations, which are spiritual combats against evils and falsities, therefore by the waters of baptism those also are signified.

5. BECAUSE baptism is for a sign and a memorial of these things, therefore man may be baptized when an infant; and if not then, he may when an adult.

6. LET those, therefore, who are baptized know, that baptism itself gives neither faith, nor salvation; but that it testifies that they receive faith, and are saved, if they are regenerated.

7. IT may hence be evident, what is understood by the LORD's words in Mark: "He that hath believed, and hath been baptized, shall be saved: but he that hath not believed, shall be condemned." xvi. 16. He that hath believed, is he who acknowledges the LORD, and receives divine truths from him through the WORD: he that hath been baptized, is he who, through them, is regenerated by the LORD. H. D. 202–208.

FROM THE TRUE CHRISTIAN RELIGION, BY EMANUEL SWEDENBORG.

8. THE First Use of Baptism is, introduction into the Christian Church, and at the same time, insertion among Christians in the spiritual world. — The Second Use of Baptism is, that the Christian may know and acknowledge the LORD JESUS CHRIST the Redeemer and Saviour, and follow Him. — The Third Use of Baptism is, that man may be regenerated. — These three uses follow in order, and conjoin themselves in the last, and thence cohere as one. T. C. R. 667–697.

CHAPTER III.

CONCERNING THE HOLY SUPPER.

And as they were eating, JESUS took the BREAD, and blessed, and brake, and gave to the disciples, and said, Take, eat; this is My BODY. And He took the CUP, and gave thanks, and gave to them, saying, Drink all ye of it: for this is My BLOOD, that of the New Covenant, which is shed for many, for the remission of sins. Matt. xxvi. 26–28.

FROM THE NEW JERUSALEM AND ITS HEAVENLY DOCTRINE, BY EMANUEL SWEDENBORG.

THE HOLY SUPPER was instituted by the LORD, that by it there may be conjunction of the church with heaven, thus with the LORD. It is therefore the holiest thing of worship.

2. BUT how conjunction is effected by it, those do not comprehend, who do not know anything concerning the internal or spiritual sense of the WORD; for they do not think beyond the external sense, which is the sense of the letter. From the internal or spiritual sense of the WORD, it is known what BODY and BLOOD signify, and what the Bread and the Wine; also, what the eating.

3. In that sense, the body or flesh of the Lord is the good of love; the bread is the same: and the blood of the Lord is the good of faith; the same is the wine: and eating is appropriation and conjunction. The angels that are with a man who comes to the Sacrament of the Supper, understand these things no otherwise; for they perceive all things spiritually. It is hence that the holy of love and the holy of faith then flow in from the angels [that are] with the man, thus through heaven from the Lord: thence is conjunction.

4. It is manifest from these things, that a man, when he takes the bread, which is the body, is conjoined to the Lord by the good of love to Him from Him: and when he takes the wine, which is the blood, he is conjoined to the Lord by the good of faith in Him from Him. But it is to be known, that conjunction with the Lord by the sacrament of the Supper is effected with those only, who are in the good of love to and faith in the Lord from the Lord. With these there is conjunction by the Holy Supper: with others there is presence, and not conjunction.

5. Besides, the Holy Supper includes and comprehends all the divine worship instituted in the Israelitish church: for the burnt-offerings and sacrifices, in which the worship of that church principally consisted, were called by one word, Bread. Hence also the Holy Supper is the completement of it. H. D. 210–214. [See also T. C. R. 698–730.]

CHAPTER IV.

CONCERNING MARRIAGE.

God created man in His image: in the image of God created He him; male and female created He them. And God blessed them: and God said unto them, Be fruitful, and multiply, and replenish the earth, and subdue it. Gen. i. 27, 28.

And Jehovah God said, It is not good that the man should be alone: I will make him a help meet for him. And Jehovah God brought the woman unto the man. And the man said, This is now bone of my bones, and flesh of my flesh: she shall be called Woman, because she was taken out of Man. Therefore shall a Man leave his father and his mother, and shall cleave unto his Wife: and THEY SHALL BE ONE FLESH. Gen. ii. 18–24.

Jesus said, He who made them at the beginning, made them male and female; and said, For this cause shall a Man leave father and mother, and shall cleave to his Wife; and they two shall be ONE FLESH. Wherefore they are no more two, but one flesh. What, therefore, GOD hath joined together, let not man put asunder. Matt. xix. 4–6.

FROM THE HEAVENLY ARCANA OF EMANUEL SWEDENBORG.

FEW know from what origin conjugial love exists. Those who think from the world, believe that it is from nature; but they who think from heaven, believe that it is from the Divine there.

2. LOVE truly conjugial is the union of two minds, which is a spiritual union: and all spiritual union descends from heaven. Hence it is, that love truly conjugial is from heaven; and that its first *esse* is from the marriage of good and truth there. The marriage of good and truth in heaven is from the LORD: wherefore, in the WORD, the LORD is called the Bridegroom and Husband, and heaven and the church are called the Bride and Wife: and on this account heaven is also compared to a marriage.

3. IT is manifest from these things, that love truly conjugial is the union of two as to the interiors which are of the thought and will, thus which are of truth and good; since truth is of the thought, and good is of the will. For one who is in love truly conjugial loves what the other thinks and what the other wills; thus also loves to think as the other does, and loves to will as the other; consequently, to be united to the other, and to become as one man. This is what is understood by the LORD's words in Matthew: "And the two shall

be into one flesh: wherefore they are no longer two, but one flesh." xix. 4–6; Gen. ii. 23, 24.

4. The delight of love truly conjugial is internal, because it is of the minds; and there is also an external one therefrom, which is of the bodies: but the delight of love not truly conjugial is only an external delight without the internal; which is of the bodies, not of the minds. But this delight is earthly, almost as that of animals; and it therefore perishes in time: but the former is heavenly, such as that of men should be; and therefore it is permanent.

5. No one can know what love truly conjugial is, and the quality of its delights, except he who is in the good of love and the truths of faith from the Lord; since, as was said, love truly conjugial is from heaven, and from the marriage of good and truth there.

6. From the marriage of good and truth in heaven and in the church, we can be instructed of what quality marriages should be on the earth; namely, that they must there be between two, — one husband and one wife; and that love truly conjugial is in no way given, if one husband has more wives.

7. That which is done from love truly conjugial is done from freedom on both sides; since all freedom is from love: and there is freedom to both, when one loves what the other thinks and what the other wills. Hence it is, that to will to rule in marriages destroys genuine love; for it takes away its freedom, thus also its delight. The delight of ruling, which creeps in in

its place, produces disagreement, and makes the minds inimical, and enroots evils, according to the quality of the dominion on the one part, and the quality of the servitude on the other.

8. It may be evident from these things, that marriages are holy; and that to hurt them is to hurt that which is holy: consequently that adulteries are profane. In fact, as the delight of conjugial love descends from heaven, the delight of adulteries ascends from hell.

9. They therefore who take delight in adulteries can no longer receive any good and truth from heaven. Hence it is, that those who have taken delight in adulteries, do afterwards make light of, and also in heart deny, the things which are of the church and of heaven. This is so, because the love of adultery is from the marriage of evil and falsity, which is the infernal marriage. A. C. 10,167–10,175.

[See also, C. L. 27–41, 45–54, 57–73, 83–102, 116–131, 156–181, 184–206, 209–230, 295–314; H. H. 366–386; A. C. 2727–2759.]

CHAPTER V.

CONCERNING WORSHIP.

Thou shalt WORSHIP the LORD thy GOD, and Him only shalt thou serve. Matt. iv. 10.

GOD is a Spirit, and they that WORSHIP HIM, must WORSHIP IN SPIRIT and IN TRUTH. John iv. 24.

FROM THE HEAVENLY ARCANA OF EMANUEL SWEDENBORG.

BY Worship, in the internal sense, is understood *all conjunction by love and charity.* A man is continually in worship, when he is in love and charity: external worship is only an effect. The angels are in such worship; wherefore with them there is a perpetual Sabbath: thence also the Sabbath, in the internal sense, signifies the LORD's kingdom. But man, while he is in the world, ought not to be otherwise than in external worship also: for, from external worship the internals are excited; and by external worship the externals are kept in sanctity, so that the internals can flow in. Besides which, man is thus imbued with knowledges, and prepared for receiving heavenly things: as also he is gifted with states of sanctity, though he knows it not; which states of sanctity are preserved to him by the LORD, for the use of eternal life: for all the states of his life return in the other life. A. C. 1618.

FROM THE DOCTRINE OF CHARITY, BY EMANUEL SWEDENBORG.

2. THE signs of charity are all the things which are of worship. All the things which are of charity refer themselves to looking to the LORD, and shunning evils as sins, and doing the goods of use which are of every one's calling.

3. BUT all the things of worship are externals of the body and externals of the mind. The externals of the body are performed by acts and by speaking; and the externals of the mind are the things done in the will and thought, which cohere with the externals of the body.

4. *The externals of the body which are of worship* are: 1, To frequent temples: 2, To listen to preachings: 3, To sing, and pray upon the knees, devoutly: 4, To partake of the sacrament of the Supper. Also at home: 1, To pray morning and evening, also at dinners and suppers: 2, To speak with others concerning charity and faith, and concerning GOD, heaven, and eternal life and salvation: 3, Also, with priests, to preach, and likewise to teach privately: 4, And with every one, to instruct concerning such things freely and sincerely: 5, To read the WORD and books of instruction and piety.

5. *The externals of the mind which are of worship* are: 1, To think and meditate concerning GOD, concerning heaven, concerning eternal life, concerning salvation: 2, To reflect upon one's thoughts and intentions, as to whether they are evil or good; and that the evil are from the devil, the good from GOD: 3, To loathe in one's mind discourses upon impious, obscene, and filthy things: 4, Besides the thoughts, there are also affections which come down to man's sight and sense.

6. THE latter things are called the externals of the mind, because they cohere with the externals of the body, and make one with them.

7. THAT such things are the externals of worship, and that the externals of worship are signs of charity, will be seen in what follows.

8. *Charity itself is in the internal man, and the sign of it in the external.* It is known that there is an internal and external man: and that the internal man is called the spirit, and the external the flesh, is also known; because it is said, and it is inly known by every one, that there is a combat between the spirit and the flesh. The spirit which combats with the flesh is the internal man which is charity.

9. THE internal man, such as it is, cannot manifest itself before the man, except through the external: when it manifests itself, there is then a combat with the external. It especially manifests itself, when a man explores himself, and sees his evils, and from thought

confesses them, and thinks about repentance, and then resists or rejects them, and strives to live a new life.

10. If a man does not do these things, his internal man is evil; but if he does them, his internal man is good. For the Lord operates through the internal man in the external; and because evil is then residing in the external, a combat arises. For into the external man, which is called the flesh, are admitted spirits from hell, who are called the devil; and the Lord in man fights with them. And if the man also fights as of himself, he conquers; and as far as he conquers, so far place is given in the external man for goods to enter. Thus a man gradually becomes new, and is regenerated.

11. Whatever the internal man produces, and presents to be seen and felt in the external, is called a sign. If charity is in the internal, it causes the man to reflect upon his evils, and actually to take cognizance of and know them; and so on. If his external does not do this, there is no sign of charity; but there is external charity without internal, which is not charity.

12. By a sign is understood an indication and testification that a thing is; because it signs and signifies, and indicates and testifies.

13. An internal without its sign as its indication is not given. If charity is in the internal man, or the spirit, and does not combat with the external man and its flesh, that charity perishes. It is like a fountain of pure water: if outlet is not given, it stagnates; and

then either its spring ceases, or the water from stagnation becomes putrid. D. C. 99–110.

FROM THE WORK ON DIVINE PROVIDENCE, BY EMANUEL SWEDENBORG.

14. FROM these things it may be evident what compelled worship is, and worship not compelled. Compelled worship is corporeal, lifeless, obscure, and sad worship: corporeal, because it is of the body, and not of the mind; lifeless, because there is no life in it; obscure, because there is no understanding in it; and sad, because the delight of heaven is not in it. But worship not compelled, when it is genuine, is spiritual, living, lucid, and glad worship: spiritual, because there is spirit from the LORD in it; living, because there is life from the LORD in it; lucid, because there is wisdom from the LORD in it; and glad, because there is heaven from the LORD in it. D. P. 137.

FROM THE HEAVENLY ARCANA OF EMANUEL SWEDENBORG.

15. IT is believed by those who do not know the arcana of heaven, that worship is from man, because it proceeds from thought and from affection, which are with him. But worship which is from man is not worship; consequently the confessions, adorations, and prayers, which are from man, are not confessions, adorations, and prayers, which are heard and received by the LORD: but they must be with man from the LORD Himself. That it is so, the church knows: for it teaches that from man not any good proceeds; but that all good is out of heaven, that is, from the Divine there; hence, also, all good in worship: and worship without

good is not worship. The church hence prays, when it is in a holy state, that God may be present, and lead the thoughts and the discourse. These things stand thus: When a man is in genuine worship, the Lord then flows in into the goods and truths which are with the man, and elevates them to Himself, and with them the man, as far and as well as he is in them. This elevation does not appear to the man, if he is not in the genuine affection of good and truth, and in the knowledge, and the acknowledgment, and the faith, that all good comes from above from the Lord. That it is so, they also who are wise from the world are able to comprehend; for they know from their erudition, that natural influx, which is called by them physical influx, is not given; but spiritual influx: that is, that nothing can flow from the natural world into heaven, but the reverse. It may be evident from these things, how it is to be understood, that the influx and operation of the Divine of the Lord is into all and each of the things of worship. That it is so, has also been often granted me to experience; for it has been given to perceive the influx itself, the calling forth of the truths which were with me, their application to the objects of the petition, the affection of good adjoined, and the elevation itself. But although it is so, still man ought not to hang down the hands, and to wait for the influx; for this would be to act as an image without life. He ought still to think, to will, and to act, as of himself, and yet to ascribe all of the thought of truth and of the endeavor of good to the LORD: thereby is implanted in him the faculty from the LORD, of receiving Him, and influx from Him. For man was created no otherwise than that he might be a receptacle of the Divine; and the faculty of receiving the Divine is not formed in any other way. The faculty being formed, he then does not will otherwise than that it should be so. For he loves the influx from the LORD, and is averse to operation from himself: since influx from the LORD is an influx of good; but operation from himself is the operation of evil. A. C. 10,299.

16. ALL external worship is a formality of internal; for internal worship is the essential itself. To make it worship from the formal without its essential, is to make the internal the external: as, for example: if one lived where there was no church, no preaching, no sacraments, no priesthood; to say that he could not be saved, nor have any worship; when yet he may worship the LORD from the internal: but it does not thence follow, that the external ought to be wanting. That this may be more plainly manifest, take also, as an example, the placing of the very essential of worship in this; that they should frequent churches, come to the sacraments, hear preachings, pray, observe the festivals, and do other things which are external and ceremonial: also the persuading one's self, (speaking about faith,) that these things, all which are formalities of worship, are sufficient. But they who make worship from love and charity essential do the like; namely, frequent churches,

come to the sacraments, hear preachings, pray, observe the festivals, and do other things, and these very diligently and carefully, but do not place the essential of worship in them. In the external worship of these, because internal worship is in it, there is something holy and living; but in that of the former, spoken of above, there is something non-holy and non-living: for the essential itself is what sanctifies and vivifies the formal and the ceremonial; but faith, separate from charity, cannot sanctify and vivify worship, because the essence and life are wanting. A. C. 1175.

[See also, H. H. 221–227 ; A. C. 1100, 1151, 1153, 1561, 1618, 1904, 1947, 2190, 2327, 7391, 7724, 7884, 10,143, 10,153, 10,203, 10,299, 10,309, 10,646 ; A. E. 325, 376, 388, 391, 401, 684, 696, 799, 942; A. R. 154, 157, 161, 859 ; T. C. R. 241, 272, 329, 354, 361, 495, 508, 667, 695, 738.]

CHAPTER VI.

CONCERNING ECCLESIASTICAL AND CIVIL GOVERNMENT.

Whoever wisheth to become GREAT among you, let him be your MINISTER; and whoever wisheth to be FIRST among you, let him be your SERVANT: as the SON OF MAN came not to be ministered to, but to MINISTER. Matt. xx. 26–28.

Render unto Cæsar the things that are Cæsar's, and unto GOD the things that are GOD's. Matt. xxii. 21.

FROM THE NEW JERUSALEM AND ITS HEAVENLY DOCTRINE, BY EMANUEL SWEDENBORG.

THERE are two things which must be in order with men, namely, those which are of heaven, and those which are of the world. Those that are of heaven are called ecclesiastical things; those that are of the world are called civil things.

2. IN the world order cannot be kept without Rulers;* who are to observe all things that are done ac-

* The word used by Swedenborg is *Præfectus*, — one who is *set over* a province or service. As we have no word so abstract, the word *Ruler* has been taken as the most general.

cording to order, and those done contrary to order; and who are to reward those who live according to order, and to punish them that live contrary to order. If this be not done, the human race must perish: for in every one it is hereditarily inborn, to wish to command others, and to possess the goods of others; whence are enmities, envyings, hatreds, revenges, deceits, cruelties, and many other evils. On which account, unless they were held in bonds by the laws, and by rewards suitable to their loves — which are honors and gains — for them that do good, and by punishments contrary to their loves — which are the loss of honors, of possessions, and of life — for them that do evil, the human race would perish.

3. THERE must therefore be rulers, that shall keep the assemblages of men in order; who are skilled in the laws, wise, and fearing GOD. Among the rulers also there must be order, lest any one from willingness or unskilfulness should permit evils against order, and thus destroy it; which is guarded against, when there are superior and inferior rulers, among whom there is subordination.

4. RULERS over those things with men which are of heaven, or over ecclesiastical things, are called Priests; and their office, the Priesthood. But rulers over those things with men which are of the world, or over civil things, are called Magistrates; and the highest of them a King, where such rule exists.

5. As regards priests, they must teach men the way

to heaven, and also lead them. They must teach them according to the doctrine of their church from the Word, and lead them that they may live according to it. Priests who teach truths, and by them lead to good of life, and thus to the Lord, are good shepherds of the sheep: but they that teach, and do not lead to good of life, and thus to the Lord, are evil shepherds.

6. Priests must not claim to themselves any power over the souls of men, because they do not know in what state the interiors of a man are: still less must they claim to themselves the power of opening and shutting heaven; since that power is the Lord's alone.*

* As an example, take the Lord's words to Peter: "Thou art Peter, and upon this rock [*petra*] I will build my Church; and the gates of hell shall not prevail against it: and I will give to thee the keys of the kingdom of the heavens; and whatever thou shalt bind on earth shall be bound in the heavens, and whatever thou shalt loose on earth shall be loosed in the heavens." Matt. xvi. 18, 19. Likewise to the disciples: "Verily I say unto you, whatever things ye shall bind upon earth shall be bound in heaven, and whatever things ye shall loose upon earth shall be loosed in heaven." Matt. xviii. 18. They who are in the sense of the letter of the Word separate from the internal, thus who are separated from the true doctrine of the Church, persuade themselves that such power was given by the Lord to Peter, and also to the rest of the Lord's disciples. Hence that infernal heresy, that it is in human power to admit into heaven and to exclude from heaven whomsoever it pleases: when yet, according to the true doctrine of the Church, which also is the internal of the Word, the Lord alone has that power. On which account, they who are in the external sense of the Word, and at the same time in the internal, comprehend that these things were said of Faith and of its

7. PRIESTS must have dignity and honor on account of the holy things which they discharge. But they who are wise give the honor to the LORD, from whom the holy things are; and not to themselves: but they who are not wise attribute the honor to themselves. These take it away from the LORD. They who attribute honor to themselves on account of the holy things which they discharge, prefer honor and gain to the salvation of souls, for which they should provide: but they who give the honor to the LORD, and not to themselves, prefer the salvation of souls to honor and gain. No honor of any office is in the person, but is adjoined to him according to the dignity of the thing which he administers; and that which is adjoined is not of the person himself, and is also separated with the office. The honor in the person is the honor of wisdom, and of the fear of the LORD.

8. PRIESTS must teach the people, and lead by truths to good of life, but still compel no one; since no one can be compelled to believe contrary to that which he thinks from the heart to be true. He who believes otherwise than the priest, and does not make disturbance, must be left in peace; but he who makes disturbance must be separated: for this also is of order, for the sake of which the priesthood is.

Truths, which are from the LORD; and that faith from the LORD, thus the LORD Himself, has that power: and thus in no wise any man. That it is so, may be evident from the representation of Peter, and of the twelve disciples; also from the signification of a Rock. A. C. 9410.

9. As priests are the rulers for administering those things which are of the divine law and worship, so are kings and magistrates for administering those which are of the civil law and judgment.

10. SINCE a king cannot administer all things alone, therefore there are rulers under him, to each one of whom is given a province of administering what the king cannot, nor is able. These rulers, taken together, constitute the Royalty, but the king himself is the highest.

11. THE royalty itself is not in the person, but is adjoined to the person. A king who believes that the royalty is in his person, and a ruler who believes that the dignity of the rulership is in his person, is not wise.

12. THE royalty consists in administering according to the laws of the kingdom, and in judging according to them from justice. A king who regards the laws as above himself, is wise; but he who regards himself as above the laws, is not wise. That king who regards the laws as above himself, places the royalty in the law; and the law rules over him: for he knows that the law is justice; and all justice, which is justice, is divine. But he who regards himself as above the laws, places the royalty in himself; and either believes himself to be the law, or that the law, which is justice, is from himself. Hence he arrogates to himself what is divine; under which, however, he must be.

13. THE law, which is justice, is to be enacted by

those in the kingdom that are skilled in law, wise, and fearing GOD ; according to which, afterwards, both the king and the subjects must live. That king who lives according to the enacted law, and therein sets his subjects an example, is truly a king.

14. A KING who has absolute power, who believes that his subjects are such slaves that he has a right over their possessions and lives, if he also exercises it, is not a king, but a tyrant.

15. THERE must be obedience to the king according to the laws of the kingdom ; nor is he to be harmed by word or deed in any manner: for thereon depends the public security. H. D. 311–325.

FROM THE WORK ON HEAVEN AND HELL, BY EMANUEL SWEDENBORG.

16. DIVINE WORSHIP in the heavens is not unlike divine worship on the earth as to externals ; but as to internals it differs. They equally have doctrines, they have preachings, and they have temples in which the preachings are performed.

17. ALL the Preachers [in the heavens] are constituted by the LORD, and thence are in the gift of preaching. It is not permitted to any one besides them to teach in the temples. H. H. 221, 226.

FROM THE TRUE CHRISTIAN RELIGION OF EMANUEL SWEDENBORG.

18. THAT divine virtue and operation, which is understood by the sending of the Holy Spirit, is, with the clergy in particular, Illustration and Instruction. The operations of the LORD, which are reformation, regen-

eration, renovation, vivification, sanctification, purification, remission of sins, and at length salvation, as well with the clergy as with the laity, flow in from the Lord, and are received by those who are in the Lord and the Lord in them. John vi. 56; xiv. 20; xv. 4, 5. But the reasons why Illustration and Instruction are with the clergy in particular, are, that these belong to their office; and inauguration into the ministry brings them with it: and they also believe that when they are preaching from zeal, they are inspired; as the Lord's disciples were, upon whom the Lord breathed, saying, "Receive the Holy Spirit," John xx. 22; and again in Mark xiii. 11: some also aver that they have felt the influx.

19. It is shown above, that that divine Virtue which is understood by the operation of the Holy Spirit with the clergy, is, in particular, Illustration and Instruction; but to these two are added two intermediate ones, which are Perception and Disposition:* wherefore there are four, which with the clergy follow in order, — Illustration, Perception, Disposition, and Instruction. Illustration is from the Lord. Perception is with man according to the state of his mind as formed by doctrines; and if these are true, the perception becomes clear from the light which illustrates: but if they are false, the perception becomes obscure; which, however, may appear as if clear, from confirmations: yet this is from fatuous light, which to merely natural sight is like

* Disposition here means "arrangement in the mind."

clearness. But DISPOSITION is from the affection of the love of the will. The delight of this love disposes. If this be that of the love of evil and of falsity thence, it excites a zeal, which outwardly is harsh, rough, burning, and fiery ; and within it is anger, rage, and unmercifulness : but if it be that of good and the truth thence, it is outwardly mild, smooth, forcible, and glowing; and within it is charity, grace, and mercy. But INSTRUCTION follows as an effect from the others as causes. Thus Illustration, which is from the LORD, is turned into various lights and into various heats; with every one according to the state of his mind. T. C. R. 146, 155.

FROM THE CANONS OF THE ENTIRE THEOLOGY OF THE NEW CHURCH, BY EMANUEL SWEDENBORG.

20. THE clergy, because from the WORD they are to teach, by doctrine, concerning the LORD, and concerning redemption and salvation from Him, are to be inaugurated by the promise of the Holy Spirit, and by the representation of its transmission : but it is received by the clergy according to the faith of their life. C., chapter on the Holy Spirit, iv. 7.

FROM THE DIVINE LOVE AND WISDOM OF EMANUEL SWEDENBORG.

21. I HAVE often wondered that the angels have such knowledge from the mere action of the body by the hands; but still it has several times been shown by living experience: and it has been said that it is thence that inaugurations into the ministry are performed by

the imposition of the hands; and that by touching with the hand is signified to communicate: besides other like things. D. L. W. 220.

FROM THE HEAVENLY ARCANA OF EMANUEL SWEDENBORG.

22. SINCE the raising up of the hand and the stretching of it out, when attributed to the LORD, as is often done in the WORD, signify Divine Power, it was even made a representative in the Jewish Church. When Moses was on the top of the hill, and lifted up his hands, Joshua prevailed; and when he let them down, the enemy prevailed: and therefore they supported his hands. Ex. xvii. 9–13. In like manner the hands were laid on, when they were consecrated; as by the people upon the Levites, Num. viii. 9, 10, 12; and by Moses upon Joshua, when he was substituted in his place, Num. xxvii. 18, 23; that power might thus be given. Hence also the rite at this day of inaugurating and blessing by the laying on of the hands.

23. FOR one to put the hand on the head when he blessed, was from a ritual received from the ancients: for in the head are the very intellectual and voluntary of man; but in the body are the acts according to them, and obedience. Thus to put the hand upon the head was representative that blessing was communicated to the intellectual and the voluntary, thus to the man himself. From that ancient time the same ritual remains even at this day, and is in use in inaugurations, and also in benedictions. A. C. 878, 6292: [See also, 10,019, 10,023, 10,076, 10,044, 9955.]

FROM THE DOCTRINE OF CHARITY, BY EMANUEL SWEDENBORG.

24. THE general good consists of these things; — that in a society or kingdom, — 1, There be what is Divine among them: 2, That there be Justice among them: 3, That there be Morality among them.

25. WHAT is Divine is there through the ministers, and Justice through the magistrates and judges, as Morality is through what is Divine and what is just.

26. *Charity in the Priest.* If he looks to the LORD, and shuns evils as sins, and sincerely, justly, and faithfully does the work of the ministry enjoined upon him, he does the good of use continually, and becomes charity in form. But he then does the good of use, or the work of the ministry, sincerely, justly, and faithfully, when the salvation of souls affects him: and as this affects him, so truths affect him; because by them he is to lead souls to heaven: and he will then lead souls by truths to heaven, when he leads them to the LORD. It is then his love to teach them sedulously from the WORD; because, while he is teaching the truths from the WORD, he teaches them from the LORD: for the LORD is not only the WORD, as is said in John i. 1, 2, 14; but He is also the Way, the Truth, and the Life; as He says, xiv. 6: and He is also the Door. Wherefore, he who enters by the LORD as the door into the sheepfold, is a good shepherd: but he who enters into the sheepfold not by the LORD as the door, is a bad shepherd; who is called a thief and a robber. John x. 1–9. D. C. 65, 66, 86.

FROM THE WORK ON CONJUGIAL LOVE, BY EMANUEL SWEDENBORG.

27. MARRIAGE is to be consecrated by a priest. The reason is, because marriages, viewed in themselves, are spiritual, and thence holy: for they descend from the heavenly marriage of good and truth; and things conjugial correspond to the divine marriage of the LORD and the Church: and thence they are from the LORD Himself, and according to the state of the church with the contracting parties. Now because the ecclesiastical order on the earth minister the things which are of the priesthood with the LORD, that is, those which are of His love, thus also those which are of benediction, it behooves that marriages should be consecrated by His ministers; and — because they are then also the heads of the witnesses — that the consent to the covenant should be heard, received, confirmed. and thus established, by them also. C. L. 308.

[See also, H. H. 213–227; A. C. 1728, 2015, 3670, 6148, 8383, 9806, 9809, 9925, 9960, 10,017; 5732, 10,038, 10,160, 10,814: 3417, 7377, 7773, 10,309; A. E. 448, 811, 31, 684, 155, 237, 333, 624, 637, 700, 659, 725, 768, 330, 685, 455, 1086; A. R. 20, 854; T. C. R. 37, 400, 403, 404, 405, 661, 114, 694, 736.]

CHAPTER VII.

CONCERNING THE ORDERS OF THE PRIESTHOOD.

HE that is GREATEST among you, let him be as the YOUNGER; and HE that is CHIEF, as HE that SERVETH. I am among you as HE THAT SERVETH. Luke xxii. 26, 27.

FROM THE NEW JERUSALEM AND ITS HEAVENLY DOCTRINE, BY EMANUEL SWEDENBORG.

THERE must be order among the rulers; lest any one, from willingness or unskilfulness, should permit evils against order, and thus destroy it: which is guarded against, when there are superior and inferior rulers, among whom there is subordination. H. D. 313.

FROM THE TRUE CHRISTIAN RELIGION OF EMANUEL SWEDENBORG.

2. THE LORD, when He was in the world, had two states, which are called that of Exinanition and that of Glorification.

3. THOSE two states are represented by various things in the universe. The reason is, that they are

according to divine order; and divine order fills all and each of the things in the universe, even to the most particular. The first state is represented with every man by the state of his infancy and childhood, even to his puberty, youth, and early manhood; which state is a state of his humiliation before his parents, and of obedience then, and also of instruction from masters and ministers. But the other state is represented by the state of the same person, when he becomes master of his own right and judgment, or of his will and his understanding; in which he has authority in his own house. The first state is thus represented by the state of a prince, or of the son of a king or of a duke, before he becomes king or duke: in like manner by the state of every citizen, before he becomes the person of a magistrate; of every subject, before he gets any office; also, of every student, who is being initiated into the ministry, before he becomes a priest; and afterwards of the same, before he becomes a pastor; and then of the same, before he becomes a primate.* T. C. R. 104, 106.

FROM THE CORONIS TO THE TRUE CHRISTIAN RELIGION, BY EMANUEL SWEDENBORG.

4. THAT anything may be perfect, it is known that there must be a Trine in just order, one under another, with communication passing between; and that this Trine makes a one: no otherwise than a column, upon which is the capital, under this the cylindric shaft, and

* See the note on page 198.

under this the pedestal. Such a Trine is man: his highest part is the head; his middle part is the body; and his lowest is the feet and the soles. Every kingdom in this emulates man: there must be therein a king as the head, besides governors and officers as the body, and the citizens with the servants as the feet and soles. In like manner in the Church, a mitred Prelate, parish priests, and curates under them.* From these things it may be observed whence it is that by *three* in the WORD is signified what is complete. Coronis, 17.

* In the third and fourth paragraphs of this chapter, the common translations are given, so far as regards the words which relate to grades in the ministry. They cannot, however, be relied on as expressing the meaning of the original. The Latin is given for the satisfaction of the reader. In the third paragraph it is: "tum cujusvis gymnasistæ, qui initiatur in ministerium, antequam fit sacerdos; et postea hujus, antequam fit pastor; et deinde hujus, antequam fit Primas." In the fourth it is: "similiter in Ecclesia, Primus infulatus, Antistites parochi, et flamines sub illis." Some think *Primus* here a misprint for *Primas.* Here is the Trine expressed in two different series:

1. Primas,	Pastor,	Sacerdos.
2. Primus infulatus,	Antistites Parochi,	Flamines sub illis.

From the use of most of these words by ecclesiastical writers generally, from the analogies of others never before used in theology, and from ecclesiastical history from the earliest centuries, it would appear that the terms in both of these series, beginning with the lowest grade, and avoiding the hierarchal terms of all sects, mean essentially, — 1, ordained and settled ministers, — 2, ordaining and overseeing ministers, — 3, a general superintendent: — that is, functions similar to those of priests, bishops, and archbishop, in those churches which are episcopal in their character. But with regard to the meaning of these two passages, opinions are not unanimous.

CHAPTER VIII.

CONCERNING THE GENERAL ORGANIZATION OF THE CHURCH.

This is My Commandment, that YE LOVE ONE ANOTHER, AS I HAVE LOVED YOU. John xv. 12.

That THEY ALL MAY BE ONE, as Thou, FATHER, art in ME, and I in Thee, that they also may be ONE IN US. John xvii. 21.

Thou shalt provide out of all the people able men, fearing GOD, hating covetousness; and from them place rulers of thousands, rulers of hundreds, rulers of fifties, and rulers of tens. Ex. xviii. 21.

FROM THE TRUE CHRISTIAN RELIGION OF EMANUEL SWEDENBORG.

IT is the like with the man of the church in the concrete or in the compound, as it is with man individual or in particular. Man in the concrete or compound is a church among many, and man in the individual or in particular is a church in every one among those many. It is according to divine order that there should be generals and particulars; and that both should be together in every thing; and that otherwise particulars would not exist and subsist: as there would not be any particular within in man, unless there were generals, by which they were encompassed. The particulars in man are the viscera and the parts of them; and the generals are the envelopments, which are not only around the whole man, but also around each of the viscera, and around each of the parts of them. It is the like in every beast, bird, and worm; and the like in every tree, shrub, and seed: nor can sound be given from strings or by the breath, unless there be something most general, from which each particular of the modulation derives its general, that it may exist. It is the like also with every sense of the body; as with the sight, the hearing, the smell, the taste, and the touch: and it is the like with every internal sense, — those which are of the mind. These things are adduced for the sake of illustration, that it may be known, that in the Church also there are generals and particulars, and also things most general; and that it is thence, that Four Churches have preceded in order: from which progression has arisen the most general thing of the Church, and successively the general and the particular of each one. In man also are two most general things, from which all the generals and each of the particulars of him derive their existence. These two most general things are, in his body, the heart and the lungs, and in his spirit, the will and the understanding. On the latter and the former depend all things of his life, as well in general as in particular;

which without them would fall asunder and die out. It would be the like with the universal angelic heaven, and with the universal human race ; yea, with the universal created world; unless all things in general, and each thing in particular, depended on GOD, His love and wisdom. T. C. R. 775.

FROM THE HEAVENLY ARCANA OF EMANUEL SWEDENBORG.

2. THE church is the image of heaven; for it is the LORD'S kingdom on the earth. Heaven is distinguished into many General Societies, and lesser ones subordinate to these: but still they are one by good.

3. WITH series it is thus. With the man who is being reformed, general truths are first insinuated, then the particulars of the generals, and at length the singulars of the particulars. Particulars are arranged under generals, and singulars under particulars. Those arrangements or orderings are in the WORD signified by bundles, by handfuls, or by collections ; and are nothing but the series into which multiplied truths are arranged or set in order. These series, with the regenerate, are related according to the arrangements of the Societies in the Heavens; but, with the unregenerate who cannot be regenerated, according to the arrangements of the societies in the hells. Hence a man who is in evil and thence in falsity, is a hell in the least form; and a man who is in good and thence in truth, is a heaven in the least form.

4. THE general things are first arranged, that into them particulars may be successively insinuated by the

LORD, and singulars into these. For, if there is not order with the generals, order cannot exist with the particulars; because the latter enter into the former, and confirm them: still less can there with the singulars; because these enter into the particulars as into their generals, and illustrate them.

5. BESIDES, it is to be known, that there must be a general, in order that there may be any particular; and that a particular can in no way exist and subsist, without a general; and indeed, that it subsists in the general: and that every particular is situated according to the quality and according to the state of the general. A. C. 4837, 5339, 3057, 4325.

---

6. THE LORD'S Church, in its most extended sense, consists of all those, wheresoever they may be, who acknowledge a Divine Being, and are in good of life according to the truths of their religion. Before the LORD they constitute ONE CHURCH: for the LORD makes one whole out of various parts; thus one Church out of many.

7. THE New Church, in its most general form in our country, consists of all receivers of the Doctrines, who live according to them. The principal of these are the "Doctrine of the New Jerusalem concerning the LORD," the "Doctrine of the New Jerusalem concerning the Sacred Scripture," and the "Doctrine of Life for the New Jerusalem."

8. THE consociated visible body of the New Church in this country, represented in the "General Consociation of the New Church in the United States," is composed of all Associations, General Societies, single Societies, and individual receivers of the Heavenly Doctrines, that are willing to unite with it, or to connect themselves with its organization.

9. THE LORD, in His WORD, has given the precept of mutual love among brethren, as the law of His Church; and this law tends to draw them together into consociation, for the exercise of this love, and for mutual coöperation and support. And inasmuch as Heaven is distinguished, according to its uses, into organizations, which, before the LORD, are general, particular, and single, the Church, which is the LORD's heaven on the earth, ought to aspire to a similar perfection of order. Where order is not, there the LORD is not; and where true order exists, there the LORD can flow in, and be present in first principles and in ultimates. Consequently it is the duty of the Church to arrange all things pertaining to its existence on earth in order: alike its general things, its particulars, and its single things.

10. THE uses of the Church, in its most general form, are the following:

I. To receive and to keep, to translate and to publish, the Sacred Scriptures.

II. To receive and to keep, to translate and to publish, the revelations which have been made by the LORD through Emanuel Swedenborg.

III. To provide for, and to regulate, the Ministry; and to establish and maintain all institutions that are necessary for this purpose.

IV. To provide for the preservation of order in the Church.

V. To provide Liturgies, Periodicals, and books of religious instruction.

VI. To send forth Missionaries and Colporters, to announce the Second Coming of the LORD, and to preach the Doctrines of His Church.

CHAPTER IX.

CONCERNING ASSOCIATIONS OF THE CHURCH.

By this shall all know that ye are My disciples, if ye have love one to another. John xiii. 35.

And he lifted up his eyes, and saw Israel dwelling according to their tribes. And he took up his parable, and said, How goodly are thy tents, O Jacob ; thy tabernacles, O Israel. Num. xxiv. 2–5.

And Moses chose able men out of all Israel, and placed them for heads over the people, rulers of thousands, rulers of hundreds, rulers of fifties, and rulers of tens. Ex. xviii. 25.

INASMUCH as heaven is distinguished into many General Societies, and into Societies of less extent that are subordinate to them, and that are still united in love ; it is proper that this order should prevail in the Church. Consequently there ought to be Associations, or General Societies, in the Church, occupying given districts within one common country, and devoted to the particular uses of the Church within their proper bounds.

2. These Associations are constituted of the Societies, Ministers, and individual members of the Church, within their several districts; who choose thus to associate, and to coöperate in the establishment of the Church. They determine their own organization and government, and modify and change the same at pleasure; being subject to the General Church only in matters touching the general regulation of the Ministry, and in the more general uses and order of the Church, as set forth in these Institutes.

3. The uses of Associations are the following:

I. To provide for the education of suitable persons for the Ministry, for inducting them into office, and for watching over them in it.

II. To send forth Missionaries and Colporters, to announce the Second Coming of the Lord, and to preach the Doctrines of the Church, within the district over which they are established.

III. To promote religious education within their respective districts.

IV. To promote social intercourse, the mutual interchange of thought and intelligence, and the cultivation of religious sympathy, among brethren of the Church.

V. To promote such other uses as may arise in the progress of the Church, or may be referred to them by Societies and individuals, in accordance with the acknowledged functions and purposes of the Associations of the New Jerusalem.

CHAPTER X.

CONCERNING SOCIETIES OF THE CHURCH.

If thy brother trespass against thee, go and tell him his fault between thee and him alone: if he shall hear thee, thou hast gained thy brother. But if he will not hear, take with thee one or two more; that in the mouth of two or three witnesses every word may be established. And if he shall neglect to hear them, tell it unto the church. But if he neglect to hear the church, let him be unto thee as an heathen man and a publican. Matt. xviii. 15–17.

HEAVEN consists of innumerable societies; and so likewise does the Church, which is the LORD's heaven on the earth. And as the societies of heaven are constituted of those who are leading the life of heaven, so likewise the Societies of the Church are to be constituted of those who are leading the life of the church; consequently, those are to be received into the Societies of the Church, who are endeavoring to conform their lives to the precepts of the WORD and the Doctrines of the Church.

2. THESE Doctrines are as follows:

I. There is one GOD. In Him is a Divine Trinity, called the FATHER, the SON, and the HOLY SPIRIT. These Three are distinct, and at the same time united, in Him; as the soul, the body, and the operation are in man: and the One GOD is the LORD JESUS CHRIST.

II. Saving faith is to believe in Him as the Redeemer, Regenerator, and Savior from sin.

III. The Sacred Scripture is Divine Truth. It is revealed to us as a means by which we may distinguish between good and evil; by which we may be delivered from the influence of evil spirits, and become associated with angels and conjoined with the LORD.

IV. We must shun evils, because they are sins against GOD, and because they are from hell; and we must do good, because it is of GOD and from GOD.

V. In abstaining from evil, and in doing good, we are to act as of ourselves; but we must, at the same time, believe and acknowledge, that the will, the understanding, and the power, to do so, are of the LORD alone.

3. OR these:

There are three essentials of the Church:

I. The acknowledgment of the Divinity of the LORD.

II. The acknowledgment of the Holiness of the WORD, and

III. The life which is called Charity.

According to the life which is Charity, every man has faith: from the WORD is the knowledge of what the life must be: and from the LORD are reformation and salvation. D. P. 259.

4. WHEN persons make a public profession of acknowledgment of and faith in these Doctrines, it is proper for them to come to the Holy Supper.

5. SOCIETIES of the Church are formed for the purpose of ultimating the principles of heaven upon the earth: and as means to this end, they are to provide for Divine Worship, for the preaching of the WORD, for the administration of the Sacraments, and for religious instruction; and also to furnish the means of doing these things.

6. SOCIETIES, in their government, and in the administration of their affairs, are bound only by the WORD, and the Heavenly Doctrines of the New Jerusalem. Each Society may determine its own government and organization, and modify and change the same at pleasure, having due reference to the larger and more general bodies of the Church.

CHAPTER XI.

CONCERNING CANDIDATES FOR THE MINISTRY.

Be ye clean that bear the vessels of JEHOVAH. Isa. lii. 11.

He whom GOD hath sent SPEAKETH THE WORDS OF GOD. John iii. 34.

He that entereth in by the door is the shepherd of the sheep. John x. 2.

CANDIDATES for the Ministry must have been received into the Church by Baptism; and they ought, above all things, to be in the life of the Church, and to have the reputation of orderly, decorous, and dignified conduct: and it is desirable that their scholarship should embrace:

I. A literary and scientific education, including a general acquaintance with the circle of Natural Science, and a competent knowledge of the Latin, Greek, and Hebrew languages.

II. A competent knowledge of the Sacred Scriptures, and of the Heavenly Doctrines of the New Jerusalem. And

III. The ability to write well, and to speak with grace and power.

2. CANDIDATES for the Ministry, while preparing for the office, may lead in divine worship, and give instruction in the Doctrines of the Church, under the direction of the Ordaining Minister of the Association of which they are members; or, where there is no Ordaining Minister in the Association, under the direction of the Presiding Minister.

CHAPTER XII.

CONCERNING THE DUTIES OF THE MINISTRY.

And He ordained TWELVE, and sent them TO PREACH THE KINGDOM OF GOD. Mark iii. 14; Luke ix. 2.

He that hath My WORD, let him SPEAK MY WORD faithfully. Jer. xxiii. 28.

A CANDIDATE, when introduced into the Ministry, is to be authorized to lead in Divine Worship; to preach the WORD and the Heavenly Doctrines of the New Jerusalem, and by means of truth to lead to the good of life; to administer the Sacraments of Baptism and the Holy Supper; to solemnize Marriages; and to officiate at Funerals.

2. A MINISTER, when installed as a Pastor, is, in addition to the powers he has before received, to be authorized to preside at the ecclesiastical meetings of the Society over which he is installed; to lead its worship; to officiate in receiving members into it; to watch over them; and to lead them in the way of life.

3. A PASTOR, when introduced into the office of

Ordaining Minister, is, in addition to the powers which he has before received, to be authorized to gather members of the Church together, and form them into Societies; to ordain other Ministers; and, when desired, to dedicate Temples and Houses of Worship; to take the general charge of the Church and its institutions, and the more particular charge of the societies which have no pastors within the district assigned to him.

4. INAUGURATIONS into the Ministry are to be performed with appropriate religious services, and by the imposition of hands, as the representation of the Divine Benediction, and the transmission of the Holy Spirit. [See T. C. R. 146, 155; D. L. W. 220; A. C. 878, 10,019, 10,023, 9955, 10,176.]

CHAPTER XIII.

CONCERNING INTRODUCTION INTO THE MINISTRY.

Ye have not chosen Me, but I have CHOSEN YOU, and ORDAINED YOU. John xv. 16.

Feed My LAMBS: Feed My SHEEP: Feed My SHEEP. John xxi. 15, 16, 17. — A. C. 4169, 10,132.

APPLICATION for admission into the Ministry is to be made by the candidate to the Ordaining Minister of the Association, with the recommendation of the Committee on Missions, or the board performing the duties of such committee, or at the request of any portion of the Church desiring his services for themselves. He is to be examined by the Ecclesiastical Council of the same; and, if approved, he may be ordained at such time and place as may be agreed upon.

2. APPLICATION for the installation of a Pastor is to be made by the Society which desires his services, to the Association within the bounds of which it is sit-

uated; and, if approved, he is to be installed at such time and place as shall be agreed upon.

3. Application for the consecration of an Ordaining Minister is to be made by an Association to the General Consociation of the Church in Convention assembled; and, if approved, the consecration of the candidate is to be performed by the President of the Consociation, or by the senior Minister of its Ecclesiastical Council, at such time and place as may be agreed upon.

REFERENCES.

[References for Chapter VIII., on Love in general, page 82. — See A. C. 760, 1055, 1589, 2057, 2041, 2146, 3338, 3736, 4776, 5130, 5807, 5949, 6872, 7081–7085, 8853–8858, 9954, 10,130, 10,177, 10,189, 10,284; T. C. R. 43, 45, 399; A. R. 691, 729, 756; A. E. 423; D. L. W. 1–3.]

[References for Chapter XI., on Faith, page 102. — See A. C. 36, 363, 364, 367, 379, 389, 654, 724, 862, 1017, 1076, 1077, 1162, 1176, 1608, 1858, 1873, 2046, 2189, 2190, 2228, 2231, 2343, 2349, 2364, 2383, 2419, 2435, 2682, 2839, 3146, 3324, 3325, 3394, 3412, 3413, 3773, 3868, 4180, 4352, 4448, 4663, 4672, 4730, 4741, 4754, 4925, 4926, 5351, 5893, 6047, 6269, 6272, 7039, 7342, 7623–7627, 7752–7762, 7778, 7950, 8033–8037, 8078, 8094, 8099, 9088, 9239–9245, 9363–9369, 10,083, 10,555; A. E. 227, 232, 242, 315, 797, 798, 815, 832; A. R. 111, 451, 483, 500, 700; T. C. R. 336–391; F. 1–72.]

[References for Chapter XV., on Merit, page 121. — See A. C. 1774, 1877, 1936, 2027, 2273, 3816, 4007, 6388–6393, 9210, 9715, 9974–9984, 10,219, 10,227; A. R. 86, 758, 854; T. C. R. 439–442, 626–666.]

[References for Chapter XVI., on Repentance, page 124. — See A. C. 8387–8394; A. E. 162, 165, 585, 589, 993; A. R. 69, 72, 379, 531, 937; T. C. R. 509–570.]

[References for Chapter XVIII., on Temptation, page 133. — See A. C. 751, 761, 762, 847, 857, 1661, 1692, 1695, 1717, 1740, 1787, 1820, 1937, 2272, 2273, 2694, 2795, 2816, 3318, 3928, 4249, 4572, 6829, 8165, 8179, 8273, 8367, 8370, 8567, 8958–8969; A. E. 631, 730, 897, 900; T. C. R. 126, 596 600.]

PART IV.

CONSTITUTION OF THE GENERAL CONSOCIATION OF THE NEW CHURCH.

PART IV.

CONSTITUTION

OF THE GENERAL CONSOCIATION OF THE NEW JERUSALEM CHURCH IN THE UNITED STATES OF AMERICA.

PREAMBLE.

WE, Members of the New Jerusalem Church, Ministers and Delegates of its Associations and Societies, and individual Members of the same, in General Convention assembled, in the city of Chicago, June 1860, do receive and adopt the "PRINCIPLES OF THE NEW CHURCH," as set forth in the foregoing *Declaration*: and we unite under the following, as the Constitution of this Consociated Body of the Church, to promote the welfare and establishment of the New Church, as the LORD's Kingdom on the Earth.

ARTICLE I.

CONCERNING THE NAME.

THIS Body shall be called "THE GENERAL CONSOCIATION OF THE NEW JERUSALEM CHURCH IN THE UNITED STATES OF AMERICA."

ARTICLE II.

CONCERNING THE MEMBERSHIP.

1. THIS Body shall be constituted of all Associations, Societies, Ministers, and individual Members, of the New

Church, who unite under this name and constitution, to promote the establishment and welfare of the Church.

2. Any Association, Society, Minister, or Member, of the New Church, not in connection with this Body, may, on application, be admitted to membership in it, by a vote of the same, when in Convention assembled.

3. The Individuals constituting the Associations and Societies of this Body are, themselves, to be considered members of the same; but as having committed to their Ministers and Delegates the right of acting and voting for them in its Conventions.

ARTICLE III.

CONCERNING THE CONVENTIONS.

1. THIS Body shall hold Conventions, annually or otherwise, at such time and place as may be determined by its members in Convention assembled, or by its duly authorized officers.

2. In these Conventions, all Ministers and Members of the General Consociation are invited to be present, and to take part in the deliberations; and the following shall be entitled to vote: Delegates from Associations and Societies; the Ministers of such Associations and Societies; and such isolated Members as are appointed to office by this Body, or to serve on its Committees.

3. Every Association or Society shall be entitled to be represented in the Conventions by its Ministers and two Lay Delegates; and every Association or Society numbering fifty members shall be entitled to three Delegates, and to one additional Delegate for every additional fifty members.

4. Every Association may send as many Delegates as the Societies constituting it are entitled to, or as many as its individual members would be entitled to, if no Society belonged to it: *Provided*, that the Delegates shall come from the Associations as such; and that Societies belonging to the Associations that are members of this Body, shall not be

entitled to be otherwise represented than by the Delegates from the Associations themselves.

5. In the Conventions of this Body, the representative, or representatives, of any Association or Society, shall have power to cast the whole vote to which its Ministers and Delegates would be entitled, were it fully represented.

ARTICLE IV.

CONCERNING THE USES OF THIS BODY.

THE Uses of this Body are the following:

1. To receive and to keep, to translate and to publish, the Sacred Scriptures.

2. To receive and to keep, to translate and to publish, the revelations which have been made by the LORD through Emanuel Swedenborg.

3. To provide for, and to regulate, the Ministry; and to establish and maintain all institutions that are necessary for this purpose.

4. To provide for the preservation of order in the Church.

5. To provide Liturgies, Periodicals, and books of Religious Instruction.

6. To send forth Missionaries and Colporters, to announce the Second Coming of the LORD, and to preach the Doctrines of His Church.

ARTICLE V.

CONCERNING THE GENERAL ORGANIZATION.

1. THE officers of this Body shall be a President, a Vice-President, a Secretary, and a Treasurer; an Ecclesiastical Council; a General Council; a Board of Finance; and such other Boards, Functionaries, and Agents, as may be appointed from time to time by the Consociation in Convention assembled, or by its authority.

2. The President, Vice-President, Secretary, and Treasurer, shall be elected triennially, by ballot; and their duties

shall be those usually belonging to these offices, and such as may be determined in the By-Laws, and in the subsequent transactions of this body.

3. The Ecclesiastical Council, the General Council, and the Board of Finance, shall be so constituted, and their duties shall be such, as are hereinafter provided for.

ARTICLE VI.

CONCERNING THE ECCLESIASTICAL COUNCIL.

1. The Ecclesiastical Council shall consist of the Ordaining Ministers, and one Pastor to be elected triennially from each Association: and from every Association consisting of ten Societies a second Pastor shall be elected; and an additional Pastor for every ten additional Societies.

2. The Duties of this Council shall be the following:

1st. To regulate the Ministry, and to provide for the introduction of suitable men into it, according to the Principles of the Church, and the determination of this Body.

2d. To provide the forms and order of Divine Worship, and the necessary Liturgies for the use of the Church.

3d. To furnish Books of religious instruction, and Periodicals for the Church; or to cause this to be done.

4th. To determine all matters of conduct and discipline that may be referred to them by the Associations and Societies of the Church.

5th. To provide for the general superintendence of the Church, and of its institutions.

6th. To provide for the propagation of the Heavenly Doctrines in districts where the Church is not yet established, and to appoint the necessary agents and functionaries for this purpose.

7th. To hold such meetings as they may determine.

8th. To address the Church annually, either by Letters, Communications, or Messengers; and to recommend to the Consociation, in Convention assembled, such measures as they may deem important, and in the interim of its sessions, to the General Council.

9th. To report their transactions annually to the General Consociation in Convention assembled, and to be subject to its control.

ARTICLE VII.

CONCERNING THE GENERAL COUNCIL.

1. THE General Council shall consist of sixteen members, of whom the President, Vice-President, Secretary, and Treasurer, shall be members *ex officio.*

2. The remaining twelve members shall be chosen to serve for three years: *Provided,* that in the first election under this Constitution, four members shall be chosen for one year, four members for two years, and four members for three years; and that thenceforward four members shall be chosen annually.

3. When the General Consociation is not assembled in Convention, the General Council shall be its organ *ad interim;* and shall have power to execute all orders, resolutions, and determinations of this Body; and to appoint such Agents, Committees, and Boards, as they may determine; and in all these matters to act with the authority and power of the General Consociation itself. And they shall report their transactions annually to this Body in Convention assembled, and shall be subject to its control.

ARTICLE VIII.

CONCERNING THE BOARD OF FINANCE.

1. THE Board of Finance shall consist of the Treasurer as chairman, and not less than one member from each Association; all of whom shall be Laymen, and shall be elected annually.

2. It shall be the duty of this Board, to collect the Funds required for carrying on the uses of the General Consociation, and to deposit the same with the Treasurer; who shall hold them subject to the order of this Body. They shall establish such agencies as may be necessary for these pur-

poses; and shall report annually to the General Council, or to the Consociation in Convention assembled.

ARTICLE IX.

CONCERNING AMENDMENTS.

The alteration or amendment of this Constitution shall require the action of the General Consociation at two successive annual meetings in Convention assembled.

ARTICLE X.

CONCERNING THE RATIFICATION.

When this Instrument shall have been adopted in Convention, laid before the Associations, and reaffirmed at a succeeding Convention, it shall become the Constitution of this Consociated Body of the Church.

www.ingramcontent.com/pod-product-compliance
Lightning Source LLC
LaVergne TN
LVHW011202110826
845150LV00006B/1299

* 9 7 8 1 4 2 5 5 1 8 8 2 0 *